Born in Dublin in 1960, Christy Dignam found his vocation to become a singer watching David Bowie perform 'Life on Mars' at the age of 13. Over more than three decades, he and his band Aslan have shared dizzy highs, crushing lows and several near-death experiences to emerge as one of Ireland's best-loved acts. Along the way, Christy and Aslan have written hit songs that, as the comedian Tommy Tiernan observed, 'have become part of the Irish DNA'.

Damian Corless has known Christy Dignam since the early 1980s when his band New Career played support to Christy's Meelah XVIII at the legendary Ivy Rooms. Damian was MTV's first Irish correspondent. He was editor of the culture guide *In Dublin* and Ireland's top current affairs journal *Magill*. He has written television comedy for RTÉ and the BBC. He is the author of more than a dozen books, and the stage comedy *Death Wish '16: The GPO*.

MY CRAZY WORLD

THE AUTOBIOGRAPHY

CHRISTY DIGNAM

WITH DAMIAN CORLESS

**SIMON &
SCHUSTER**

London · New York · Sydney · Toronto · New Delhi

First published in Great Britain by Simon & Schuster UK Ltd, 2019
This edition published in Great Britain by Simon & Schuster UK Ltd, 2020

1 3 5 7 9 10 8 6 4 2

Simon & Schuster UK Ltd
1st Floor, 222 Gray's Inn Road
London WC1X 8HB

www.simonandschuster.co.uk
www.simonandschuster.com.au
www.simonandschuster.co.in

Simon & Schuster Australia, Sydney
Simon & Schuster India, New Delhi

A CIP catalogue record for this book
is available from the British Library.

Paperback ISBN: 978-1-4711-8433-8
eBook ISBN: 978-1-4711-8432-1

Typeset in Palatino by M Rules
Printed and bound by CPI Group (UK) Ltd, Croydon, CR0 4YY

I want to dedicate this book to my beloved Kathryn,
without whom I would not have been around to write it.

CONTENTS

PROLOGUE

This is What They Have for You When You're Dead

FRIDAY 21 JUNE 2013, THE OLYMPIA THEATRE DUBLIN PRESENTS 'A NIGHT FOR CHRISTY'

Featuring Mary Black, Paul Brady, Jedward, Horslips and many others. Special appearance by U2 live from New York.

The big night arrives and a car is sent to pick us up. We pull up at the stage door of the Olympia Theatre and the laneway is jammed with happy well-wishers milling around. I've never seen anything like it in all my years playing.

I've always wondered what it would be like to be in the audience for an Aslan gig and now it's happening. There I am sitting in one of the boxes, looking at the crowd gathered below, and on the stage there's a big backdrop with an image of me and the words: 'A Night For Christy'. And then it strikes me. *That's* what this is. *This* is what they have for you when you're dead.

Everybody wonders what it would be like to go to their own funeral and to see who'd turn up and what they'd say about you. This was me getting the chance to go to my own funeral!

Then, as it was drawing to a close, U2 came on live-streaming from New York with a powerful performance of 'This Is'. They did a brilliant version, putting their own stamp on the song we wrote.

I kinda cried my way through that gig – it was really emotional. The crowd were looking up and clapping when there'd be little waves to me from the performers on stage. My grandson Cian was there to take it all in. It was one of the nicest experiences I've ever had from music, after all the compromises and bullshit the business puts you through. More than any other in my entire career, *this* was the golden moment to treasure.

1

A Picture-Perfect Childhood

Finglas sprawls from the edge of Glasnevin Cemetery into open country, which is as alien as open sea to city-bred residents. Finglas West is still in a state of explosion, at a point of uncertain development. This uncertainty is not helped by the fact that, although sixteen years old, Finglas West has only recently acquired adequate street lighting, shopping centres and bus services.

Horizon, Telefis Éireann, January 1968

I was born Christopher Patrick Dignam on 23 May 1960 in Dublin's Holles Street Hospital. My da, also Christopher Patrick, was reared in Dominick Street, just off O'Connell Street in the very heart of Ireland's capital city. When my da was a youngster his family moved out to Cabra, not much more than a mile away but then on the outskirts of the city limits. My ma was Theresa Kavanagh, the first born of what would be six children. Because she was the eldest, she was sent off to live with her granny from the time she was really small, because her mother had other babies coming along in quick succession. When her mother and her siblings came to visit my ma as a young girl, she would always be wearing a lovely dress, and her brothers and sisters were jealous of her fine clothes. But as soon as the visit was over, the nice dress was ripped off her and she'd be put back to doing the horrible jobs that her granny made her do. For instance, she'd be made to clean in between the bannisters of the staircase with a toothbrush. One day she left a finger stain on one of the bannisters and her granny threw a beer bottle at her that smashed on the back of her head. My mother stayed with her granny until she was thirteen years of age, when her own mother brought her back home to take over the minding of her five siblings.

After she was back home a year or so, my ma was coming home from school one day when she passed her mother in the street. My ma was fourteen years of age, and she was now effectively running the household. As they passed each other, her ma said, 'Will you fix the kids their dinner? It's in the oven.'

She assumed her ma was going to the shops, but instead she fucked off to England. The mother was finally leaving the father who was a terrible alcoholic.

So my ma was left rearing her five younger brothers and sisters on her own. A pattern developed. As each of the siblings reached fourteen or fifteen – old enough to start earning a living – the mother who'd run off would send for each of them in turn to come over to England to get a job. Over the course of time all of my ma's younger brothers and sisters ended up in the English Midlands. With the last of them gone, my ma could finally concentrate on getting a life of her own.

My ma Theresa and my da Christopher grew up on opposite ends of Cole's Lane, which was just off Moore Street. Like Moore Street it was full of market stalls selling fruit and veg, shoes and second-hand clothes. They never knew each other as kids, but they finally met at a dance after my da's family moved to Ballybough and my ma would regularly visit family in that part of the north city. They fell in love, got married and moved into her family home in Cabra, where she was now the only one left, minding her alcoholic father.

The young couple had my older sister, Bernadette, and then they had me. The trouble was, every time one of ma's siblings would have a row with their wives or husbands in England, they'd come home and move straight back into the place where they'd grown up. For my ma and da, trying to mind two babies and a sickly man, the stress was terrible. The father, my grandfather, drank himself into an early grave and my ma's mother arrived back in Cabra for the burial. They were obviously very poor because the neighbours had to do a whip-around to pay for the funeral. That didn't work out too well. My granny robbed the collection money and fucked off back to England with it! My granddad is buried in a pauper's grave somewhere – we could never find it.

The constant comings and goings of my ma's brothers and sisters in and out of the house in Cabra finally got too much for my folks. My da said enough of this, and he got us a house in Finglas. Dublin's urban sprawl was starting to gather pace, and Finglas was the last outpost of the spreading city before you reached endless countryside.

I admired my ma for her unbreakable spirit. For her, life

just sent one trial after another. Years after she had last been seen – doing a runner from her own husband's funeral – my granny turned up at our house looking for help. She'd been hit by a motorbike crossing a road in Coventry when she was in her seventies and had to have a steel hip replacement. So she came to live with us in Finglas to convalesce for a few months. She ended up convalescing there for the next fifteen years! So that was my ma's life. As just a little toddler she was sent to live with a wicked grandmother. Then, when she was finally brought home, it was only as a workhorse, to raise her younger siblings. No sooner were they all reared than she started rearing all of us, her own children, and as soon as we were all grown she was back caring for her prodigal mother again. From the age of fourteen until her mid-sixties my ma was either rearing or caring without a break.

My brother Eddie was the last born of our family, nineteen years after the oldest, Bernadette. He brought the total number of children to eight. In between came me, Deirdre, James, Thrêse, Brian and my youngest sister Jackie. When Eddie was born we went into the maternity hospital to visit my ma, and the doctor called in my da. The doctor told him, 'Your wife is forty-six years of age and this is her eighth child. She nearly died this time with toxaemia. I do not want to see that woman in here again. Have you never heard of contraceptives?' Of course everyone had *heard* of contraceptives – you just couldn't get them because they were illegal.

My da used to go to the dogs every Saturday, and one Saturday when my ma was in hospital having Edward, I was out on the town with all my mates. We'd been having a wander around the Dandelion Market, and when the stalls packed up we went to Peter's Pub for a few drinks. Peter's Pub was just across the way from the Gaiety Theatre and, as we passed the Gaiety, I saw my da's car parked outside. I thought to myself, my da's doing the dirty on my ma! I was heartbroken at the thought. Since I was little he'd always gone greyhound racing at Shelbourne Park on a Saturday, and now I was wondering if it was a front all those years.

The following Saturday he was leaving the house and I asked where he was going. He said he was going to the dogs. He drove off and I followed him, a teenage Columbo on a Honda 50! I tailed him all the way to Shelbourne Park and watched him go in. Nothing suspicious there. When he got home that night I asked him if he'd won anything. He said he hadn't. I asked if he'd won anything the previous week. He said, no, he hadn't gone the previous week. He'd gone to the Gaiety with a mate of his from work. I felt such a dick. To this day I still don't know what I was thinking.

Many years later, when my granny died, I went with my ma to the morgue in Blanchardstown Hospital. My ma was looking at her lying there. I put my arm around her to comfort her and she said in hushed tones, 'I *hated* that bitch.' A strong thing to say about your mother when she's lying there in front of you, but that woman crucified my mother. By rights, my ma should have been a bitter, twisted woman given the life she'd had, but she wasn't. She was an amazing woman. And my da was an amazing man. Eight kids in a small house – how did they do it?

Far from being crushed by the hands she'd been dealt by

life, my ma was a real jovial person. These days if you're play-ing football and the ball bursts you go to Smyths toy shop and get another one. Back in the day, if you burst your ball you heated a kitchen knife until it was red hot, you melted the plastic to seal the hole and you pumped the ball back up. When I was a kid, when anybody burst their ball on the road, or got a puncture on their bike, or their chain came off, it was straight up to my ma's and she would fix it. She was the go-to mechanic on the road. She was a great mother and a great woman.

The Finglas I grew up in was completely surrounded by fields. At the end of our road there were sports grounds, but after that it was just countryside as far as the eye could see. We played football and chasing on the streets, and all the other games kids used to play outdoors because all the mothers were very house-proud and they didn't want any horseplay indoors messing up all their neat housework.

We used to go nesting birds up the fields. When I was nine, ten, twelve years old, that was my passion. Nesting birds meant finding the nests. You would never take the eggs out of the nests – we were eco-friendly before anyone ever used that term. You'd have common birds like blackbirds or jackdaws or magpies. Finding their nests was par for the course. The glory came from finding the nests of the kingfisher or the goldcrest – that's a tiny bird like a wren with a little flamed crest on its head. They're very rare, and if you found one of their nests you'd get great kudos from the others.

Today I have bird feeders in my back garden, which is just a few miles from where I grew up, and you'll see the odd blue tit, maybe a greenfinch here and there, but what you mostly see are sparrows. The variety has gone. When I was a kid we'd set traps – a box propped up with a stick attached to a wire. You'd throw a handful of seeds underneath the box and wait, pulling the wire to spring the trap when there was a bird under there. You'd have hundreds of goldfinches, bullfinches, chaffinches, every bird you could imagine, because we were so near the countryside. You do that today, in Finglas or anywhere in Dublin city, and all you get is sparrows.

My love of birds has stayed with me all my life, and today I breed native finches. A few years back, when I first got very ill, I decided I should get rid of the birds because my health was going downhill and I knew I'd soon be too sick to take care of them. I was also afraid that keeping birds might make me even sicker, because there's a mite you can get from feathers. Around that time, a young girl in Dublin working in a pet shop had a bad reaction to this mite and she died. When I was first getting trouble with my health, and before I'd had the diagnosis of cancer, I thought it might be to do with all the shit and dust I was inhaling when I'd be cleaning out the birds. I investigated and discovered that you only get this particular mite on parakeets, but this was still playing on my mind when I decided to get rid of the birds.

I brought them to the bird market in the Liberties area of Dublin and put them on sale. Bride Street Market near St Patrick's Cathedral has been the place to buy and sell birds in Dublin for hundreds of years. Go in there at ten o'clock any Sunday morning and you'll find huge numbers of them in cages hanging from nails on the old wooden doors.

Everyone's heard of the greenfinch, but there's a mutation called the cinnamon greenfinch and they are rare and really expensive. The morning I brought my birds to market, this young fella comes up to me and he has a few coins and he says, 'Mister, how much is them greenfinches?' He's pointing at my cinnamon finches. He has about 30 cents in his hand and these things cost at least 150 quid for a pair. But I looked at him and said, 'These are the last two. You can have them.'

He looked at me with disbelief.

'Are you serious, mister?'

'Yeah, I'm serious. They're yours. Take good care of them.'

And he runs off, thrilled with himself.

About a week later I was down in the dumps and missing my birds and thinking I should have kept a couple of them. So I decided to go back to the market and get just a single pair, which I reckoned I'd be able to mind.

I went in and, straightaway, I saw a pair of cinnamon finches. *Bingo!* So I bought them for 150 quid and handed them to my da and my son-in-law Darren, who were sitting outside in the car. I was heading back into the market to see what else was there when they beeped the horn and waved me back. I went back to the car and they said, 'C'mere, look at the ring on this bird's leg.' It read 'C.D. 2013' – Christy Dignam, 2013.

They were my birds! The ones I'd given to this kid for nothing. The bastards had sold them back to me for 150 quid! I probably could've found the kid again, but I admired his entrepreneurial spirit.

To explain – there's a law now against catching native

birds in the wild, like we used to do as kids, which is a good thing because all our songbirds are disappearing. If you're someone like me, who breeds native birds, you have to attach these tiny closed rings to the hatchlings' feet twelve days after they hatch. This means that if the ISPCA (Irish Society for Prevention of Cruelty to Animals) raided the aviary they'd be able to see straightaway that the birds aren't caught birds, but ones I'd bred myself.

My da encouraged my love of birds by building me my first aviary at the back of our house. My love of singing also comes from my da. He's still alive and almost ninety, and he's a great father and a great man. He was an upholsterer. He upholstered cars and buses and household furniture. He worked with Peugeot in Sallynoggin, and for a few other smaller places. When I was a kid he upholstered the carriage of the Lord Mayor of Dublin. He worked for the transport company CIE for thirty years, upholstering the buses. All our chairs at home were covered in greeny-blue bus seat upholstery. When I was in my mid-teens, all my mates would be in the house watching a match on the telly, and when the game was over I'd say, 'Okay, let's go outside.' And they'd all make out they were stopping the bus to get off, pulling this imaginary chord on the ceiling: 'Ding! Ding!' So that gave me the opening line from our first hit single, 'This Is' – 'These are the hands of a tired man', as my da's hands were all calloused and hard from his work.

My da gave us a very healthy disregard for religion as we were growing up. When he was a kid, his ma would always have a shilling put aside for when the church helpers came around knocking door-to-door for the parish dues. Even if there wasn't food in the house she had to have that shilling for the church collection. This went on through all the years he was growing up.

When my da's father died, the family rang the priest to come to the house to anoint him. The priest told them that the cost of getting the deceased anointed was half-a-crown. My da's mother, who'd scrimped to pay her parish dues every week without fail, told the priest she didn't have the money. The priest refused to come to the house to anoint her husband. For my da, that was the straw that broke the camel's back as far as the church was concerned, although much later in life I'd learn about his terrible treatment when he was put in the care of the Christian Brothers because the family no longer had a father.

As a kid myself, I had other things on my mind than religion. I spent my childhood Saturdays in the Casino, our local fleapit cinema. Once a year this act called Coco the Clown would come to the cinema, and instead of a film he'd make funny balloons and stuff. I remember when the first *Batman* movie with Adam West and Burt Ward came to the Casino in 1967, and the queues went around the block. I'll never forget when Superquinn next door expanded and took over the Casino and turned it into part of the supermarket. As a young kid I thought it was the worst thing in the world.

A lot of our childhood activities revolved around the WFTA, the West Finglas Tenants' Association. They had a committee that ran football road leagues for under-10s, under-12s and so on. If you were a boy growing up in Finglas in the 1960s or '70s, football was a big part of your life, mostly because there wasn't much else to do.

My dad was very affected by the Munich air disaster, which wiped out Manchester United's golden generation of 'Busby Babes' in 1958. As a kid, he'd bring me up to visit the grave of Liam Whelan in Glasnevin Cemetery. Whelan died in the air crash at the age of just twenty-two. He was the only Irish Busby Babe and he was from Cabra. But just because I was brought to visit Liam Whelan's grave didn't mean I grew up supporting Manchester United. The two big rivals of my childhood were Chelsea and Leeds, so I followed Chelsea and hated Leeds. I don't actually hate any team or any person, but when you're ten years old a lot of things in life are black and white. The player I hated most was the Leeds forward Allan Clarke because he represented that 'Roy of the Rovers' stereotype of clean-cut English heroism, and he was *so* hero-worshipped by the English. He was the Harry Kane of his day. I gave up on supporting Chelsea in the early 1990s when there was a big scandal involving a Tory minister caught with his trousers down in a Chelsea shirt. That part of the story later turned out to be fake news, but at the time it was the final straw. I'd always supported Celtic along with Chelsea, but ever since then I've only supported the team from Glasgow.

Finglas and Cabra have produced some great footballers. When we were kids, I played for Cardiffsbridge and Ronnie Whelan played for Abbotstown in the road leagues. Ronnie would end up a legend, winning six league titles and the European Cup with Liverpool. That was never on the cards

11

for me. I played as a forward but I wasn't very good. I used to slide into puddles and muddy patches on the logic that the more covered in muck I was coming off the pitch, the more people would think, wow, he must have had a great game! One year, Cardiffsbridge met Abbotstown in the final of the West Finglas road league and they beat us two–nil. Ronnie Whelan scored both their goals, so even at the age of ten or eleven he stood out. But I had a friend, Mikey Hewitt, who lived across the road from me. Mikey and Ronnie played for the same team at Home Farm all the way from the under-10s up. Another mate of mine, Gary Howlett, who would play for Brighton in the 1983 FA Cup Final, was a year or two behind them. When Mikey was around twelve years of age, he was invited to go over to England for a trial with Arsenal. His da said he was too young, but he'd let him go if they sent another kid over with him. So Ronnie Whelan was sent as that other kid.

Mikey was brilliant with both feet but when he went over there he just couldn't hack it being away from home. Mikey came back to stay and, in the years when he should have been knuckling down to football, he got into teenage distractions. We're still great mates. You have to hand it to Ronnie – he turned out a great player but Mikey walked rings around him back then. Mikey became a groundsman at Shelbourne FC's home, Tolka Park, just a few miles from where he grew up. Today he drives a courier van for a living. You don't know where life will take you.

On Sundays during the summer, the West Finglas Tenants' Association would put on buses to the seaside. There might be four buses collecting people from our road. Everyone from Cardiffsbridge would meet at the top of our road, everyone from Mellows would meet at the community centre on Mellows Road, the people from Deanstown would meet for the Deanstown bus, and so on. This would be a family day out, which meant the *whole* family; the dads weren't allowed to skive off to the pub for the day. All the mothers and fathers would have to be there to control their own bundle of kids.

On a Sunday morning this fleet of buses from Finglas would head off for the north Dublin beaches of Rush or Portmarnock or Skerries or Dollymount. We'd all pile out onto the beach and the WFTA would boil up all these big kettles for making tea. The communal spirit was brilliant back then. Finglas was a young, vibrant place at that time with young marrieds and lots of kids, and everyone had this belief in a bright future.

Even the journey back from the seaside was a laugh. There were a few serious boozers on every road, and they'd be singing all the way home. There were a lot of football anthems sung. My dad never drank, but I loved the antics of the other oul fellas off the road. The father of a mate of mine was a mad gargler, and on those bus journeys back from the beach I used to say to myself, Jesus, I wish my da was like him. On days like that it felt like a picture-perfect childhood. You couldn't ask for any better.

2

The End of Innocence

I had a lovely childhood. As far as I was concerned, it was a perfect childhood. Until ...

When the story first came out in the papers in 1988, about me being strung out on heroin, I went straight to the Rutland Centre in Dublin to sign myself in. I'd known for some time that I had to go in anyway, but when all the publicity blew up it was like, well, it's all out in the open now, so I can go in. So I did.

When I entered the Rutland I was the only heroin addict in there. They didn't really do heroin addiction at that time. I think I was the first. There were a lot of alcoholics and gamblers and people hooked on prescription medication. I'd be in the class and I'd say, 'My name is Christy. I'm a drug addict.'

Then this girl would say, 'My name is Mary. I'm chemically dependent.'

And I'd say to her, 'So, you're a better class of junkie than me.'

There was a bit of that snobbery.

In the fourth week, nearly to a man and a woman, all the others would have an epiphany, like, 'When I was twelve my dad used to come home from work every night and beat the shite out of us.' They all had these horror stories.

And I had nothing.

They'd try to drag it out of me in one-on-one counselling, but I couldn't find anything. I kept insisting there was nothing wrong with my life; that I had a perfect childhood. I was thinking about my da building the aviary for us. He did everything for us. And our mother did everything that could be expected of a mother.

After I left the Rutland Centre I went up to visit my ma and da for Sunday lunch, as I did from time to time. On one particular Sunday I said to her that I'd learned in the Rutland that maybe my addiction was to do with something that happened to me as a child.

My da gave me this look that said: 'Are you saying to me that I didn't hug you as a child?' He didn't speak those words out loud, but his look said exactly that.

I left the house thinking, fuck, I'm after making the whole bad situation even worse. That's not what I was trying to say at all. So I'm walking out of the house disgusted with myself. My head is wrecked. And I'm passing this neighbouring house and I look at the front door, and *THUD!* – the whole thing comes back to me. Oh fuck!

It all flooded back. When I was around six, this guy sent me up to the van for a bottle of Pop Cola. I didn't know much about him, except that he was sixteen or seventeen and he didn't have a job. His mother and father went out to work during the day. He had one sister, who worked, so he was always in the house on his own during the day.

Pop Cola was real cheap stuff. Thousands of people had been moved into the newly built estates of Finglas West before the authorities had put in even the essentials like shops and a bus service, so there were van shops that sold the basics like bread and milk and sweets. You'd get threepence from your ma or da for going to the van to get messages. I went to the van for the Pop Cola and got back to the neighbour's with the little bottle, and the hall door was open a fraction, so I knocked on the door.

His voice came from behind the door saying to bring it in.

I entered, and I'll never forget the slam of the door behind me and the dead bolts going *Clang! Clang! Clang!*

The curtains were pulled, so we were in darkness. He grabbed me and shoved me and stripped me and took the laces out of my shoes and tied me to a chair. He then took out his dick. It was the first time I'd ever seen a mature dick with all this hair. It frightened the shit out of me. He got me to toss him off and all that fucking carry on.

When it was over he told me not to tell anybody. Those dead bolts clanged again and I was out into the brightness. When I reached my mates out on the road they were asking me where I'd been, and I remember lying to them, saying I'd been in my own back garden. Before that I'd told lots of little white lies about all sorts of things, like all children do. But this was like the first real lie I'd ever told. Something changed that day. I was never the same after that.

It happened a few more times. I'd be at the door and he'd drag me in. Not *literally* drag me in, though, because if I'm honest – and this is what caused me so much trouble later on – I felt kinda chosen. Of all the kids on the street he picked *me*. So I didn't mind going in, whereas I thought I should have been disgusted. That caused me a lot of mental turmoil later on in life – the guilt of not feeling horrified by it.

I don't know how often it happened, or how far apart the incidents were. I just know it happened over a period of time. And then it stopped.

I told no one. I didn't understand what had happened but I did know that it was a secret, and that keeping the secret was very important. He got that message into me because I was left feeling that I'd done something wrong. I think he paid me sixpence that first day, instead of just the threepence for getting him the Pop Cola, so I kinda felt that I got paid for it as well. There were all those things chasing around in my head that I didn't understand.

I found out later he was doing it to a couple of other kids on the road. Years later this man came up to me who I'd known when we were kids, and he told me he was having trouble with his wife – that he couldn't perform sometimes. He said, 'I think it's because what happened to you happened to me too.' This was shortly after I'd revealed the abuse in the papers.

'It was such-and-such a person, wasn't it?' he said.

I said yeah, and he said, 'He did the same to me.'

He told me, 'Sometimes I'll be with the wife and I can't get a horn.'

And that made me remember my own times when I'd be with a girl, telling myself, see, Christy, there's nothing wrong with you. You're with a girl! My sexuality was totally messed up.

I had no big brothers to stand up for me. I was the eldest

boy in the family. I had friends who were younger kids in their families, who had big brothers to stand up for them. The abuser didn't do any of those kids. He knew who to pick. He had an antenna for it.

Then the abuse just stopped. I didn't say anything about it and nobody knew anything about it. But then, when I was about nine years old, I told a mate of mine.

'C'mere,' I said. 'You know so-and-so? You know what he did to me a few years ago?'

The friend came back to me a couple of days later and said he'd been talking to his older brother. The brother would have been about the same age as the guy who'd abused me three years earlier, and would have known him. My mate says, 'My brother can help you. He knows how to help you and he wants to talk to you when he comes home from work.'

So that night I went around to my mate's house and we went up to the brother's bedroom. The brother told my mate to wait downstairs because we had things to discuss that we didn't want to air in front of him.

So there we were, me and the older brother in the bedroom to talk through the abuse I'd suffered, and he did the fucking same thing to me!

That really compounded in me that I had some responsibility in it. I was three years older than when it first happened, and I had a little more savvy than when it happened before. This time I *knew* there was something bogey about it. I knew to avoid the brother from then on and I didn't let it happen again.

When you're a drug addict, at least for *me* as a drug addict, you have this gnawing inside you, this hunger, this hole to fill. That hole was born the day I was first abused in that darkened house, a few doors down from the love and safety of my own home, when I was six years of age. I remember that darkness coming into me.

When I look back at my childhood, it's all visions of running through fields of barley; it's all a joy, until I come to that day it all turned.

When I was lying in a hospital bed a few short years ago, and told I only had days to live, I had plenty of time to rewind over my life. I tried to go back as early as I could, and I was lying there on that bed smiling at how good life was as a really young kid. And then this shadow came over me, like I was dead. It was really strange. You can look at what happened on an intellectual level – and tell yourself that what happened happened and you're not to blame – but that doesn't matter because the damage is done. For him, that first abuser, what he did to me in that room would have been one orgasm for him – one single sexual thrill that was over in one moment – but the damage it has done … If you look at the ripple effect, the damage done to me, and as a result to my wife, to my child, to my grandchildren, to the band – the damage it has done, just for one poxy orgasm.

3

School's Out, and In, and Out

I went to Naomh Feargal primary school in Finglas, and when it was time to go to secondary school there were two alternatives in our neck of the woods. There was the Patrician College, run by the Christian Brothers, and there was the Tech, the technical school. Every single one of my mates went to the Tech, which had a gym and did sport, woodwork, mechanical drawing, all those practical kinds of things. Patrician was all academic stuff like Latin, French, Biology and the rest. My da made me go to the Patrician because he thought I'd get a better education. I can understand his reasons now, but at the time I just thought, *aw no*.

I'd never mitched from school a day in my life up until then. All through primary school I was always near the top of the class without having to make any real effort. But from the time I started in secondary I just mitched constantly, because I hated it. I used to go on the bounce from Patrician on a Tuesday, and I'd go up to the Tech where my mates would be in this mechanical drawing class where 'Moonhead' Muldoon was the teacher. I'd stand outside the classroom smoking cigarettes and handing them in through the window to my mates in class. One day, as I was leaning

20

halfway through the window, handing in a cigarette, one of my mates grabbed me and shouted to the teacher, 'Mister Muldoon, he's trying to get out the window!'

The teacher stormed down the classroom, dragged me in through the window, sat me down at a desk and warned me to never try that again. From then on, every Tuesday I'd go on the bounce from Patrician and climb through the window of the Tech and sit at a desk for mechanical drawing because all my mates were there. I might be the only schoolboy in history who's mitched from one school to sneak into another. The trouble was, I wasn't getting credits on my Patrician attendance record for turning up at a different school.

I knew that all this absenteeism would come to a head, so one school term I got up early every morning waiting for my report to come through the letterbox, because I knew there'd be a note on it about my attendance. Officially, as far as my parents were concerned, I'd missed one or two days of school. But that term I'd been out more like ninety days. So every morning I'd be first down to check the post, and then back to bed. Of course, Murphy's Law said that the one morning I slept in would be the morning the report arrived.

I was woken up by this yell up the stairs from my ma: '*Christopher!!!*' And I knew, I *knew* before I got down the stairs what it was. She battered me around the house. My ma was the disciplinarian of the household. As young kids we'd be messing upstairs when we were supposed to be going to sleep and you'd hear a shout coming up through the floor: 'You'd better be quiet up there or I'm coming up.' Then, if you heard the sitting-room door open downstairs, you'd go quiet and listen. My ma's knee joint used to crack on the stairs, so if we heard a crack we'd jump into bed and pretend to be asleep. If we didn't hear the crack we'd know it was my da and we'd all just keep messing.

My da would never, never touch us – until the day that report card came through the letterbox. He came in from work at teatime, got a talk from my ma, and I'll never forget the battering he gave me that night. I remember that battering mostly because that just wasn't him. I'd pushed him too far.

My da was a real softie in the best sense. He was a great father who led by example. He used to work every weekday and do overtime on Saturdays. And when he got home from work on Saturdays he'd do stuff for us. As I've already said, he built me an aviary for the birds I'd catch with my box-traps. On Sundays he'd make the dinner, and he used to make lovely apple cakes. And while he was making dinner he'd sing all these operatic songs by John McCormack and Enrico Caruso. Before I ever heard pop music, light opera was the first music I heard. It was listening to my da singing those songs that gave me a love of music and made me want to be a singer.

As a very small kid I joined the school choir and I sang all through primary school. Then – and this is very politically incorrect now – this girl Tony Wade started up a black and white minstrel troupe. There were about thirty girls in it, and me and my mate Ray. We did all these talent contests from a very young age. To this day when I'm singing is when I'm at my happiest. It's when I feel most at home. I believe we all have different parts to us. A little effeminism maybe, or little traits that we might be embarrassed about if they were exposed to the world, but when you're in a band and you've got that alter-ego situation, you can be all those traits. You can be a little bit effeminate, you can be a little bit stupid, you can be all these different parts of yourself. And it helps to release the demons. It exorcises all the demons.

My da was a lovely singer until he got polyps on his bowel and they put a tube down his throat to check it out and the instruments scratched his vocal cords. After that he could never sing, and it killed a lot of his joy in life. I can imagine what it did to him. Many years later I found myself in that same awful place, but we'll get to that in good time.

For now, it's back to happier days when my da was in full voice belting out the operatics while cooking Sunday dinner. When we'd finished eating he'd drive us all to the seaside at Portmarnock or to the Phoenix Park. We had a Ford Escort and there would be eight kids and my ma and da all squashed into this tiny car. I was saying to him just the other day, 'I don't know how you got ten people into that little car.'

He reminded me that three or four of the kids would be in the boot.

If the weather wasn't fine for an outing, he would bring me into town on Sundays and I loved to watch old Hector Grey in action. This big fat man was a living legend. Hector Grey's shop on Liffey Street was the best shop in Dublin as far as every kid in the city was concerned. It was packed to the ceiling with cheap toys and novelties and bric-a-brac. Often you couldn't get into his shop it was so packed, so on Sundays he'd also have a stall at the Ha'penny Bridge close to where he had his shop.

Everybody used to talk about him being a multi-millionaire, and that he was Ireland's richest man, and I used to think about that watching him do his sales pitch every Sunday. Even years later I'd think about how he'd be there every Sunday morning rain or shine, this big fat man trying to sell a couple of pounds' worth of shit stamped with 'Made in China', and there he was, a millionaire.

4

Black and White to Colour

I remember when I was about twelve, sitting in the house on a Saturday night with my ma watching snow on the telly from about nine o'clock until around eleven when the TV closed down. The ancient movie *Dracula* from the 1930s was on HTV, beamed over from Wales, and we could get the sound but not the picture. So we sat there for two hours, myself and my ma, just listening to the movie and watching black and white dots of snow.

Around the same time, colour TVs were just coming onto the market, and a mate of mine, Gerry Galvin, told me his family had got one. This was a big deal, because while everyone had heard of colour tellies no one had actually seen one. So I got Gerry to open his family's sitting-room curtains a bit that night, and the whole road was in his front garden looking through the window. After all that it turned out it wasn't even a colour telly. They'd got one of those big green magnifying-glass screens that you'd attach to the front of the set. It just made the picture bigger, and green, and distorted it like you were looking into a fishbowl, but to us it was still an improvement.

Then, when the real colour TVs did become available, the

first one in our neck of the woods was in the Cardiff Inn on our road. I remember one evening we were playing football in the street and one of the neighbours passed by on his way home, and he was in a great mood. He worked on the buses and he'd stopped in at the Cardiff for his usual after-work gargle.

He says, 'I'm after been sitting at the side of the pitch at Old Trafford – and the fuckin' size of the pitch!'

So we're just looking at him, pretty sure he had not just come from Old Trafford.

'Yeah,' he says. 'A colour telly. They've got a colour telly in the Cardiff Inn. It's like sitting in Old Trafford.'

It was a long time before anyone had colour in their house. A lot of houses had no TV at all. We had a black and white set, and we could get fairly good reception from Northern Ireland of the BBC and UTV. I remember a couple of girls off the road used to come to our house every Thursday to watch *Top of the Pops*. They were older teenagers and my ma would put it on for them. I was a bit younger than them, but I used to watch it with them, and there were a few songs I'd latch on to, like 'You Can Do Magic' by Limmie & Family Cookin', and stuff by Diana Ross, and The Stylistics, who were huge for a short time.

Then David Bowie came along and just blitzed me. I saw him doing 'Life On Mars' on *Top of the Pops* and everything changed. Everybody from that time says it was Bowie doing 'Starman' that changed their lives, but for me it was seeing the video for 'Life On Mars'. I went out and bought the single and played it to death. The B-Side was 'The Man Who Sold The World'.

Shortly after that I started listening to Bob Dylan. It was like being exposed to two totally different aspects of the music experience. Bowie was part of that glam/progressive thing, but Dylan showed me that you could write a song with a lyric that was social commentary. Bowie was the spaceman, Dylan was the reality man. That said, although Dylan had a huge effect on me, it was nothing compared to Bowie.

Slade had six number one hits when I was in my early teens and they were a fixture on *Top of the Pops*. I loved them because they were loud and raucous and they looked like pop stars should look. I remember the exact day when this bloke said to me, 'You do know that Slade are from a run-down place called Wolverhampton in England. They're from a place like Finglas.'

This was something I hadn't known and it really struck me, because I'd grown to that stage thinking that God had appeared to Mick Jagger, David Bowie and Noddy Holder and told each of them, 'You're a rock star. And you're a rock star. And you're a rock star.' I thought you had to be divinely anointed. I thought you had to be *born* a rock star. When I realised these people chose it themselves and then made it happen, that was a *huge* revelation for me. I thought, I'm from Finglas, Finglas is like Wolverhampton, and I can do this. My mistake, at that young age, was to think it would just happen because I wanted it to happen.

When I got a little bit older I realised that wanting to be a singer doesn't make you a singer – you have to put in the work, and do this and do that, and all these logistics have to come into play to achieve that goal. Before that, I thought if you wanted to be a bus driver you became a bus driver, and if you wanted to be a singer you became a singer.

5

Bath Nights and Turf Wars

> Successive governments had embarked on a programme of
> knocking down slums and sometimes transplanting entire
> communities into new housing estates. The outdoor swim-
> ming pool was seen as a way of siting cleanliness next to
> Godliness at the heart of these new communities. Known as
> the Cabra Baths, the swimming pool on the border of Cabra
> and south Finglas was of the windblown open-air type,
> freezing during the winter but merely bracing on an Irish
> summer's day.
>
> *Hopscotch and Queenie-i-o,* Collins Press, 2016

There used to be a fight every summer for control of the
Cabra Baths between the Cabrarians and the Fingallians. On
balance, there was probably more fighting took place there
than swimming. Cabra Baths wasn't a proper swimming
pool like the heated indoor ones you have today. It was a
pool built on a natural bend in the Tolka River, and the river
supplied the water as it ran through.

There was this bloke called John McLoughlin, who was
famous in Finglas. He had these white Alsatians and every
year he'd bring them down to the fight for the Cabra Baths.
It wouldn't be just one battle; it was a war that would go on

for weeks. It would just kick off for no particular reason. Word would go round town: 'The fight's on tonight.' The Cabrarians would be on the Cabra side of the Baths and we'd be on the Finglas side, and we'd be throwing rocks across the pool at each other. Or if there were one or two or maybe three kids from Cabra in swimming, you might sneak down and ambush them. The skinhead thing was big at the time, but I wasn't attracted to that and I was too young anyway. I was never in a gang like that. I did read the football hooligan books that were really big at the time, like *Skinhead* and *Suedehead*, but that was as much interest as I had in gang stuff.

I used to swim in the Tolka River upstream from the Baths at the Finglas end. There were three areas of the river where the current slowed and it was safe to swim: the Sweeps, the Scouts and the Silver Spoon. One afternoon I'd been swimming all day and, treading water, I felt this moss under my feet. It was really soft and fluffy and felt gorgeous, and I rubbed my feet on it for ages. And I thought I'm going to get that, so I reached down and grabbed it up to the surface – and it was a dead dog! I'd been swimming in this all day! And you're wondering how did we survive it? How did we not all get diphtheria?

So Finglas 'owned' that upstream part of the river and the Cabra crowd 'owned' the Baths, but we still fought them for it. We'd have control of the Baths for a day or two, and then everyone would go home when it got late. Then maybe they'd come up to the Baths in force early the next morning, and they'd beat us off when we arrived and have it for a day or two.

There would be a truce on Saturdays and Sundays in the summer because those were the days when families took over the Baths. There was a ceasefire, not just because everyone's ma and da was there, but for the simple reason that when you're all in swimming, nobody knows who's from Finglas and who's from Cabra anyway.

The Baths were filled in and covered over when I was in my early teens and there's a field there now where they used to be.

6

Will You Go with Me, Kathryn?

I first met my future wife when I was nine years of age. Her name was Kathryn Harris, and when she came down to our road those first times she had on a little pair of skates with steel rollers, and she'd go *clink-dink-dink-dink* as she was walking. She must have been hanging out with someone on our road because she lived on Mellows and I was on Cardiffsbridge, so we were about five minutes from each other.

I asked her to go with me, even though we were too young to have a girlfriend/boyfriend thing – we didn't even know what that was at that time. I was hanging around with this guy called Ray Tyrrell. He's passed away now, Lord have mercy on him. Ray asked Kathryn to go with him as well, and she said that she wouldn't go with either of us because that would mean hurting the other one. That laid down the gauntlet.

Kathryn disappeared from my life shortly after turning down Ray and me. She was still living only five minutes away but I didn't see her for years. Then, when she was thirteen or fourteen, she became friends at Mater Christi Secondary School with a couple of girls that hung around with us, so she started coming around our way again. I was about fourteen by then as well, and I remembered her straightaway as that lovely girl with the skates that I used to like. From then on I made sure to grab her attention any chance I got.

At first there was a big gang of us hanging out around Finglas Village and all walking home together for our tea. Eventually the gang thinned out, and after a few weeks it was down to just me and Kathryn sitting on a wall talking. We got to be mates before we were boyfriend and girlfriend. Five years after I asked her the first time, I asked her again: 'Will you go with me?' and that was kind of it. The first time I kissed her I knew it was different from any kiss I'd had before. We were now going out but we were also becoming best friends. We did everything together. If I wasn't at her house, she was at mine.

I don't know what Kathryn saw in me. I thought she was lovely to look at, because when you're that age the physical attraction is the first thing that matters. But very quickly I found there was something beautiful inside her. There was something about her that I 'got'. A year or so went by, and one day we were up the end of my road and she had this little blue Triumph Twenty bike with small wheels, like a Raleigh Chopper but not nearly as cool. We were going to her house, and she was doing these circles on the bike as I was walking, and I said to her, 'Kathryn, I think I love you.'

I was fifteen. Growing up, you never know what love is, but at that age you think about it a lot. How do you know when like turns to love? Is there a single moment when that happens? When is that moment?

I said the words and it was like a weight lifting. It was like I'd been carrying something for ages and, by saying those words, I'd gotten it off my chest and I was floating on air. And I absolutely believed it. I wasn't just saying it.

Kathryn said nothing. She kept cycling in little circles around me. She didn't say 'I love you' back. I was a bit *aaw*, a bit deflated.

What I was expecting was: 'Jaysus, *about time* you said it. I love you too!'

But that's not what happened.

I had to tell Kathryn I loved her that day because it genuinely struck me that friendship had turned into love, but I think there was something else to it as well, because this was almost exactly the same time I decided I was going to make my life in music.

After I started going with Kathryn, the thing that made me stay with her was her absolute support for and belief in everything I was doing to make it in music. Years later, during the deep recession of the 1980s, I gave up a permanent and pensionable job with Telecom Eireann to go full-time in a band that might never make it, and Kathryn supported me fully.

We had just married when I left my Telecom job, and the two of us had been inseparable for nine years, apart from one very short period where we split up. I still vividly remember that time. We were about eighteen, and it had been all off between us for about two weeks. I was sitting in a car outside my house smoking a joint with a mate when Kathryn appeared up the road, walking in the direction of my house.

She'd come to see me. To this day I will never forget her at that moment. She looked devastated. She looked really thin. She looked as if she'd been crying for two weeks. I can still feel how horrified I was that I had inflicted this much pain on Kathryn.

I hadn't finished with her for any kind of valid reason. I finished with her because I was eighteen years of age, we'd been together since we were fourteen, and I thought the grass might be greener on some other side. I was looking at all my mates going off with different women, and I thought that was a great place to be. I was still a kid and my head was all over the shop. Looking out the car window at Kathryn walking towards us I felt like a complete scumbag. I got out and brought her into the kitchen and asked her if she'd give it another go. She said okay.

I called up to her house later that day, thinking everything was fixed now and back to normal. Her ma grabbed me and said, 'If you ever put my daughter through that again, I'll swing for you!' Kathryn's ma was a real lady, but she told me she'd swing for me and she'd hang for me, and she meant it.

'Okay, Bessie,' I told her. 'Message understood.'

Kathryn was the baby of her family of ten kids, so maybe that's why her mother was so protective, but it was a very tight-knit and caring family anyway, and she was raised with that nurturing character. Everything I thought about Kathryn's caring nature from the first time I knew her was confirmed in later life. When her father got cancer, she cared for him like a husband for the last two years of his life. Then her mother got ill with dementia and she was there for her all the time to the end. She has the heart of a lion and I don't know how she does it. I've often thought about what would have happened if the roles had been reversed in our relationship and she was the addict. Would I have been able to put up with what she put up with? In all honesty I don't know that I would have, because I put her through some bad shit. I never raised a hand to her or anything like that, but I wasn't there for her. I made her promise after promise that I never delivered on.

Many, many years after that telling off from Kathryn's ma, we were playing a gig in Terenure, on the south side of Dublin, and I was just after coming off the gear. When you're on heroin you don't really feel anything emotionally because it's like an anaesthetic. Then, when you come off it, all these emotions you haven't felt in a long time come rushing back with a vengeance. Your nerves are raw and the least little thing makes you cry.

We were doing 'Crazy World' and we got to the chorus, 'How can I protect you . . .' and I looked at Kathryn standing behind the mixing desk, and I said to myself, you *haven't* protected her, you cunt. I completely lost it. I had to get off the stage. I gave Billy this pleading look, trying to get him to take over the song.

When we got back together after those two weeks apart, we got engaged. We were still only eighteen yet other people were getting engaged at sixteen and seventeen. Getting engaged very young was the done thing in parts of Dublin, but up until then I had no intention of it because at that age you don't know if the mot you're going out with is your *real* mot. Even though I knew I loved Kathryn, I didn't know if she was the one. She was the one for now. I know that sounds cold, but at the time we were still very young and I didn't know any better.

7

Knock, Knock, Knocking on Joe Jewell's Door

Joe Jewell was in my class right through primary school. He was in the choir as well, so I've known Joe since I was seven or eight years old. We wouldn't have mixed early on, but I'd have been vaguely aware of him as someone around the place. I remember being at a party in his house after the school choir sang at his brother's wedding. That was back at a time when newlyweds had their wedding reception back at their family home.

Years later, in our teens, Joe was a member of a band called Electron, made up of blokes from Patrician College, my school. They split up and I knocked down to Joe's house one Friday and told him I wanted to start a band and I'd like him to play guitar. He said, 'Knock back to me next Friday.' So I knocked back to him the next Friday and he said, 'Knock back to me next Friday.' And this went on every Friday for six months.

'What about now, Joe?'

'Ah no, not now. Knock back next Friday.'

The main reason I kept turning up at Joe's front door

Friday after Friday was because he was the only musician I knew. I kept knocking on his door with no success until one day in 1976 or 1977 when he told me that Electron were reforming for a once-off gig in The Towers pub in Ballymun, and that I could be the singer. In addition to Joe himself, the band had another guitarist called Martin Meagher, and Terry McFarland was the drummer. Martin was a ridiculously good guitarist compared to Joe, and he soon moved on to Rocky De Valera and The Gravediggers, who were a happening band in the late 1970s. But Joe was gifted in other ways. Joe would work out harmonies for songs. He'd know why a certain thing wasn't working musically – stuff I wouldn't have a clue about. I knew what sounded good in my ear, but Joe could tell me *why* it sounded good. He'd tell me that I was trying to sing a minor over a major chord and that's why it jarred. I also had this idea that great rock bands are made up of partnerships between the singer and the guitarist, like David Bowie and Mick Ronson, Mick Jagger and Keith Richards, even Simon Le Bon and Andy Taylor of Duran Duran. I saw Joe in that light, as someone I could collaborate with. So, as far as I was concerned, myself and Joe *were* the band. Everybody else was peripheral.

The gig in The Towers was a benefit for the Irish Youth something-something-something. It was actually an IRA fundraiser, though we didn't know that until we got there.

For the next three weeks we rehearsed like mad. Our whole set was covers. We did songs by Bowie, Thin Lizzy, Bob Seeger, that kind of stuff.

The big night came and we went on stage at The Towers.

Joe and the others had all played live before but this was my first time going out in front of an audience. I remember standing there, looking out at all these faces, and holding the mic so tight that I could see my knuckles trying to burst through my skin. I was literally scared stiff. I didn't move an inch off that spot for the whole night.

We finished the set after what seemed an eternity. But I'd got through it and the ordeal was over. Except it wasn't. The organisers came up and told us that we had to finish up with 'Amhrán na bhFiann' ('The Soldier's Song'), the national anthem. 'Amhrán na bhFiann' was the theme tune of the 1916 Easter Rising. It was sung by the rebels holding the General Post Office against the British, and was a favourite in the republican internment camps that followed.

A lot of the men out there in the audience were now standing to attention with their black berets and their James Connolly badges. This was their song. And, of course, we didn't know it. We didn't know the national anthem.

I was fucking terrified. We were all fucking terrified.

'Whatcha mean you don't know the fucking national anthem?!'

I can't remember how we got out of that situation. I think we just legged it. And we didn't do another gig for about a year afterwards, after barely escaping with our lives. We were that traumatised.

After being frozen to the spot for that entire first gig, I came up with a clever plan. I found that if I closed my eyes so I didn't have to look at the audience, I was able to walk around the stage. The trouble with my clever plan was that, because I had my eyes shut, I kept tripping over the leads and gear strewn across the stage. The solution to my solution was to take my shoes off so I could feel my way around the stage floor.

Before long, what started out as a cure for tripping over turned into a superstition. In the same way that footballers will always put a boot on one foot first, or have to be the last one out of the dressing room, I was afraid to do a gig with shoes on. I'd be thinking, no, I won't be able to sing wearing shoes. For a long time I performed on stage in my bare feet. Many years after that first gig in Ballymun, I remember being on stage in Donegal on an icy winter's night and my feet were like blocks of ice, but I continued through to the end because I was convinced I wouldn't be able to sing with my shoes on.

Our disaster with the national anthem aside, myself and Joe took enough encouragement from our first show together to try something more permanent. We rehearsed, and wrote some original material, and eventually launched Electron on the pub circuit. Our first proper gig was at The Magnet on Pearse Street supporting a new-wave outfit called the Myster Men. That introduced me to the Dublin music scene and I started going to see alternative punky bands like DC Nein. The gigs I loved most were by the likes of The Outcasts and Rudi, who both came down from Belfast. I loved the rough and ready Northern Irish punk thing because we were just finding our way and learning how to play, and the punk thing gave us an entry point into this world of the gigging circuit. The trouble was that a lot of the punk style was screaming and shouting and, before long, I started wearing down my voice, and my range was getting shorter. I felt I had beautiful music in my head but I wasn't getting it out. I'd started out with a fairly good voice but now I was actually going backwards and doing it physical damage. That freaked me out totally, and that's when I started looking for a good singing teacher to try to get my voice back.

I tried loads of singing teachers who weren't much use before I found this guy called Frank Merriman who had a place over Walton's music shop just across from the Garden of Remembrance on Dublin's Parnell Square. All the teachers I'd been to before had been dismissive of rock'n'roll. They told me if that's the way I wanted to go I was wasting my time and their time. My response to that was: 'Fuck you, I'm a rock'n'roll singer!' Frank had no problem with me being a rock'n'roll singer. His attitude was that there are only two types of singer – good ones and bad ones. So Frank introduced me to the *bel canto* method.

Bel canto means beautiful voice in Italian. It comes from the monks of the sixteenth and seventeenth centuries who would sing all day. The problem with all that singing is that eventually your voice will seize up. So the monks devised a method where the more you sang, the stronger your voice got – if you did it properly.

Over time the *bel canto* method migrated from the monasteries to the great opera houses of Italy and Europe. The teachers were now great maestros and they would make a huge investment in their pupils. They would pick their singers as young boys and train them for five or six years. When the singers were fully trained they began to earn a living, and the maestros were on a percentage of their earnings. So if a maestro didn't produce a great singer, that meant the singer wasn't in demand and the teacher had wasted five or six years training a dud. This in turn meant the teacher had to choose his singer with great care, because he would be putting massive belief into the chosen one, and in that student's willingness and ability to learn. So when someone like Frank puts his belief in you, and thinks you're good enough to do it, this instils in you the belief that you're good enough to do it. Frank himself had been picked by one of these maestros and became a fantastic opera singer, until diphtheria wrecked his voice and his career. Fortunately for me, and a lot of other singers, he came back to Ireland and started teaching. Sinéad O'Connor, Samantha Mumba, Boyzone and Christy Moore are just some of the people who've learned from him.

One of the first things Frank said to me was that before he could teach me how to sing, he was going to un-teach me. He explained that every singer who comes to him, myself included, arrives sounding like someone else. Every singer naturally absorbs the mannerisms of people they've been listening to. We develop a liking for the way certain people sing, for their inflections and their idioms. You might like the way Bowie sings the words 'car', 'window', 'boat', or how Mick Jagger sings 'tree', 'bush', 'aeroplane', and you end up building a vocabulary of other people's idioms, but all the time you're losing your own essence as a singer. So you have to strip away all that stuff you've robbed and get back down to what makes you you. The only unique thing you have to offer the world is your own personality. It's also worth remembering that as much as a Damon Albarn or a Bob Marley sound exotic to us, an Irish accent sounds just as exotic to them.

So the very first thing Frank taught me was that the world already had a Mick Jagger, and the world already had a David Bowie, but what the world had yet to hear was a Christy Dignam. Hearing that from your teacher really makes you believe in yourself! From the very start with Frank I knew that he could teach me to express the sincerity I've always felt within me through my vocal cords, turning a feeling into a physical expression. That's what *bel canto* is all about. It doesn't matter whether you sing or you play the tin whistle. What matters is whether you're using the instrument with sincerity, because people recognise sincerity and that's what they relate to and love. Frank taught me so much. He's the best.

8

Lazing on Those Sunny Afternoons

In May 1977 Ireland's first McDonald's opened on Dublin's Grafton Street. It became the general HQ of the fledgling music scene, with U2 and countless other wannabe rock stars holding court. McDonald's was a stone's throw from the epicentre of the capital's teen social network, the Dandelion Market, on what is now the Stephen's Green Centre. Like a fabulous oriental bazaar, the stalls, kiosks and cubbyholes of the Dandelion sold everything your parents would hate. It had ripped punk T-shirts, hippy joss sticks, trippy posters, badges, belt-buckles, lava lamps, miles of vinyl and far-out stuff like Patchouli Oil and twenty types of chickpea mush. Rumour had it that you could even buy a pile of illegal stuff under the counter, including condoms.

Irish Independent

In the late 1970s we'd get the 40a bus from Finglas to Parnell Street and walk up to Grafton Street just to taste a McDonald's burger. McDonald's was the first branded burger to come to Ireland. There were plenty of existing burger joints, but to me they all had the same taste. They all tasted like the Granby burgers your mother bought in the local butchers, and they all had lumps of gristle in them and a

45

spicy-ish taste. They were probably good burgers, but compared to all the others McDonald's burgers tasted like steak. And now I taste a McDonald's burger and it's horrendous. I wouldn't buy one now.

McDonald's wasn't just the first branded burger, it was one of the first brands to come to Ireland. Before that, brands didn't matter to Irish people. Now, brands seem to be all that matter.

On Sunday afternoons you'd go up Grafton Street and there would be absolutely nothing open except McDonald's. But then you'd get to the top of the street and there, opposite the front arch bringing you into Stephen's Green, was the bustle and colour of the Dandelion Market. You'd get stuff there that you'd never see anywhere else. I got a pink vinyl copy of 'Q: Are We Not Men? A: We Are Devo!', and various other coloured discs and picture discs. Discovering weird and wonderful stuff at the Dandelion was a huge chunk of my youth.

The Boomtown Rats were making it big in Britain around that time and their keyboard player Johnnie Fingers had a sister who owned a shop called No Romance, just up from the Dandelion. It sold all punky gear. I bought a coat there and it was the most horrible-looking thing you've ever seen, but because I'd bought it in No Romance I thought it was great. You could get stuff there that you couldn't get anywhere else, if you could afford the big price tags.

Every Saturday afternoon myself and Timmo, the band's drummer, would go to the Dandelion and check out whatever bands were playing the car park. Those car park gigs have gone into legend as the ones that gave U2 their start. Usually it was local bands that had a bit of a following, or were being built up as maybe the Next Big Thing. A lot of times you'd come away saying, 'I could do better than that.'

9

Drunken Sailors, Beauty Queens and Mincing Cigarettes

When I left school in the mid-'70s there wasn't a lot of work out there, and because of that it was no big deal for lads to spend their days rehearsing in a garage. To this day I believe a recession is good for music. It frees people up but it also fires people up, especially working-class people, about the injustices going on in the world. It's healthy in that way.

Today the pressure is on youngsters to get a job or, if they can't get a job in Ireland, to get out of the country and get a job in Australia or England or America. In the 1970s people felt no shame about not having a job. The great thing about that situation was that your parents allowed you to rehearse your music. I remember getting my first little PA system. My ma went in and paid it off at £4.95 a week for nearly a year. It was a shitty PA but it was great of her. That's how supportive she was.

You weren't being pushed into a job because there usually wasn't a job there. Economic stability wasn't a big deal if it wasn't an option. When we were kids we went to the soup kitchen behind the Bottom of the Hill pub in Finglas for our dinner. Not every day, but the odd day. We'd get a bowl of stew and a lump of bread cut from a batch loaf. And for an extra ha'penny you'd get semolina – known to us as salmonella. I used to love the soup kitchen, being at the long table. All the tramps would be eating there but you didn't give a fuck. There was no shame in it.

When I was ten I went up to Downes Bakery in Finglas village very early one Saturday to look for a job. Someone had told me to arrive there at six o'clock in the morning and sit where the bakers' delivery vans were getting loaded up with bread and cakes. If a van boy didn't turn up you'd be there to take his job for the day delivering bread. The very first time I did this I got a van and I ended up staying with the same van until I was around eighteen. I became friends with the breadman, and even if there was no work for me I'd hang around for the vibe.

I'd get one pound, one Irish punt, in wages for doing the bread deliveries and out of that I'd give my ma half, leaving 50p for myself. One year I saved my 50ps for fifteen weeks to get a Wrangler jacket that cost £7.50 from O'Connors of Middle Abbey Street. Things like that you saved for, but today 10-year-old kids have to have Adidas and they expect to be handed the money. I bought those Wrangler jeans when I was around fifteen years old, and by that age you were expected to go out and earn your own money. Your parents weren't going to be buying you Wrangler jeans or Adidas runners.

One of my first jobs after finishing school was working in the Player Wills cigarette factory. I was recently looking at an old photo from my Players days and the sleeves on my jumper were almost up to my elbows because it was a hand-me-down that I'd had since I was ten. That wasn't a big deal. We were less materialistic in those days. We're extremely materialistic now and that makes us slaves to the economy. The whole spirit and soul of the country has changed in that respect, and not for the better.

I went onto the Player Wills cigarette factory floor aged fifteen or sixteen straight from the Inter Cert, which would be the equivalent of today's Junior Certificate. Players operated a system where you did six months on the workforce, and then you were kind of sacked. Twenty people taken on in the same batch would be let go at the same time six months later. Then the five best workers among them might be taken back on and given permanent jobs.

I was on this contraption called the slitter, which was like a huge meat-mincing machine with a conveyor belt coming out of it. They had a big barrel on wheels, the size of a fridge, full of loose, stale, out-of-date cigarettes. The slitter was to recycle stale tobacco. They'd mix a pound of old tobacco from our machine with a stone weight of good fresh tobacco and send it on to be repackaged as all good tobacco.

My job was to wheel this barrel over to the slitter, tip it over and shovel all the cigarettes into the top of this machine. Next you turned on the machine and all the minced cig-arettes started coming out onto the conveyor belt, and my job was to crouch over the moving belt and – *whish, whish, whish* – pick out all the shreds of white paper as they passed. Mental! One tiny sliver of paper would get by you and you'd jump to try to get that, but then all the others would be backing up behind it. There would be me and one other guy doing this, and the conveyor belt didn't stop. One of us would be shovelling in the cigarettes and the other picking out the little bits of cigarette paper. It was a nightmare.

I swear there were times I'd be sitting on the number 22 bus coming home from the South Circular Road and a scrap of bus ticket would flitter past and I'd jump out of my seat to go for it!

My nerves were shot from the job. It's inhumane, hovering over a moving line trying to pluck out tiny bits of paper. So I would get steel bolts, and I'd throw a bolt into the slitter. That would wreck the blades and the engineers would have to come down and it would take them an hour to fix the thing. Just to give you a rest!

When my six months was up and I was laid off with all the others, I had no intention of ever going back into that, even in the unlikely event they offered me the permanent job.

From as early as I can remember I always wanted to be a singer, but I didn't realise that to make that a reality you had to get a band together. All through school I was thinking that learning all these subjects isn't really necessary because I'm going to be a singer, but I hadn't worked out how I was going to achieve that.

I was still trying to work this out after I left the cigarette factory around the age of sixteen, when I landed a job with Irish Continental Lines on the *Saint Patrick* ferry going from Rosslare in County Wexford to Le Havre in France. There'd be a lot of schoolkids on board coming and going on school tours, and if we had a bad sea they'd be puking up everywhere and you'd be going around after them with a bucket and mop. It was a horrendous job.

I only lasted a short while on the ferries. I was a galley boy, so my job was to help the chef. On my first day on the ferry the chef told me that if I didn't do my job the right way the kitchen staff wouldn't report me to the pursers, they'd take me up on the car deck and give me a few slaps.

I was there a couple of weeks and I was up on the car deck, talking to the guys that worked there, and they were all huge dockers. One of them asked what did I think of the job, and I said I thought it was a great job except for the threat of getting a beating on the car deck. The dockers said this sounded a bit rough, and asked me to explain about the punishment beatings on the car deck.

That night, I was in bed when there was a knock on my cabin door around four in the morning. I dragged myself out of bed, opened the door and the chef was standing there bollock-naked, soaking wet and purple with the cold. The lads from the car deck had stripped him and stood him on deck for an hour and now they'd brought him down to apologise. He'd made up all that stuff about the punishment beatings just to get me to do all his work as well as my own. He had me peeling potatoes and doing all the scabby tasks that he was supposed to do, and which had nothing to do with my job description.

Between leaving one port and docking at the other, there wouldn't be much to do, so the crew would be up to all sorts. The captain of a vessel traditionally had a ship's cat living in his cabin. So one night, again around four in the morning, they had me knocking on the captain's door with a saucer of milk because they told me it was the cat's feeding time. The captain nearly threw me overboard! Another time they had me going out on deck with a brush to clean the black tar off the funnel in a force eight gale. I'd have been blown back to France if I'd actually tried it. There was a lot of that sort of messing.

Even when you had time off in Le Havre you wouldn't get out of the docks. You might take a walk, but you'd only get as far as one of the pubs. The first time I went for a wander the only drink you could get anywhere was Heineken, and that was really exotic because the only lager you could get in Ireland was Harp. It seemed like it cost about 100 quid for a bottle of beer on French soil, whereas duty-free drink was there for next to nothing on the boat.

It seemed to me that nearly all the crew on the boats I worked were alcoholics, and a lot of them were big gamblers. The reason for both was that once you finished your shift there was nowhere to go and nothing to do. It was all mad gargling and playing cards. You did two weeks on and a week off, so a lot of people were drunk on duty all the time.

The best thing about working on the ferries was that the wages were great. The average wage in Ireland would have been about twenty quid a week for a young fella my age, and I was on about thirty-five quid a week. That was huge money, and you couldn't spend it because you were away at sea two weeks out of every three. You'd come home at the end of two weeks with seventy quid in your pocket and you were rich.

The coming home rich part was great, but I quit because I didn't like the being away from home part, and the longer I spent at sea taking home great money, the further I was from doing what I should have been doing, which was singing. The way the ferries worked, it was now a case of trying to track down Joe every three weeks instead of every week. The logistics of it were just too much.

So I left the ferries and got on a government work experience course. Some bloke came in looking for people to do suspended ceilings, so I went with that and I ended up putting in ceilings for four or five years. About three years of that was spent doing the ceilings of just one huge building – the Allied Irish Bank headquarters opposite the RDS in Ballsbridge. I did the National Irish Bank in Booterstown, then I did the ceilings in the old Finglas Garda Station.

I was in the Garda Station one day, and when you're panelling the ceilings the method is that you work yourself into a corner. Knocking-off time arrived at five, but I'd only a single block of the ceiling left to do, maybe ten tiles, so I decided I'd finish there and then instead of having to face it in the morning. But it took longer than I thought, and it came to after six o'clock and I was still there. Next thing – *boom, boom, boom* – the room is full of cops running at me from both doors. They thought I was after breaking in through the roof. Very embarrassing.

Synchronising my working hours with Joe's meant we'd both be free to rehearse at the same time, so when he got a job in the national phone company, Telecom Eireann, I joined Telecom Eireann too.

If that makes it sound easy to get a job in Telecom Eireann, it wasn't. It was hard. Lots of people applied for every vacancy because it was a good, pensionable state job and you needed to have a great Inter Cert and all that carry on. I got in and became a telephone technician installer, so I used to work on the underground cables.

One job was on Sydney Parade in Sandymount, in a very well-heeled part of Dublin. We had a machine called a tapper that you attach to the cables to isolate where the fault is. But this day my work partner had forgotten to put the tapper in the van and he had to drive back to the base in the city centre to get it. He told me to stay there by the manhole, which we hadn't opened yet. So I'm sitting there on the wall of this gaff by the train tracks on Sydney Parade when I hear this police siren in the distance. And I'm thinking they must be chasing a stolen car. That's the sort of thing you hear in Finglas all the time, but it's not what they'd be used to over in Sandymount.

The sound of the siren is getting nearer and nearer until this police car swings around the corner and starts flying in my direction. And I'm thinking, Christ, what's happening here? Next thing this squad car screams up to me, screeches to a halt, pins me against the wall and these cops jump out and grab me. It turns out I was outside a judge's house, walking up and down, loitering, and they thought I was casing the place to rob it or maybe kidnap the judge! The Troubles were at their height and there were a lot of kidnappings going on.

At this time we were going along pretty aimlessly with Electron. We used to play beauty pageants in a country club just outside the city limits. We'd be playing the Miss Finglas beauty contest and the promoter would give us fifty tickets and tell us that if we sold the fifty tickets he'd let us play the pageant. In our innocence we thought this was great, but we were making a fortune for the promoter for the privilege of playing for free. All our gigs were shit gigs, and we were still playing Thin Lizzy covers. In fact, all we played was covers. Watching bands playing their own songs at the Dandelion Market, I realised that we'd go nowhere until we started writing our own stuff. So we transitioned from Electron, the covers band, to Meelah XVIII, which would play original material.

We took our new name from the novel *Mila 18* by Leon Uris. Mila 18 was the address of an apartment in the Warsaw ghetto during the Nazi occupation of Poland. It was a HQ of the resistance fighters. We decided to pick a name after a book because that seemed like the cool thing to do. To me at the time, finding the right band name was harder than writing songs.

10

Should I Stay or Should I Go?

Kathryn's da was on the committee of WFTA, the West Finglas Tenants' Association. They ran bingo nights, those much-loved bus trips to the seaside, the road football leagues where I played against Ronnie Whelan and a whole range of other community activities. They would go to Spain every year and I thought they must be millionaires because nobody in Ireland went on sun holidays in the 1970s.

But Kathryn told me it was all down to getting the numbers. All her sisters and brothers would go, and there were about ten of them. People would try to rope in neighbours and relations. When you had enough people, the Association could charter a plane to Spain and book the rooms, and because you were doing it on that scale it was really cheap. And because it was Kathryn's da putting the whole thing together, I jumped at the chance to go to the sun. I'd never been abroad. I'd had one or two holidays as a child with my parents, but never out of the country.

One was to the seaside in Tramore, where loads of Dublin families still go every year. Another time we went to a place down in Kilmuckridge in County Wexford. I was aged about ten and I set the place on fire. It was a farmhouse holiday on a working farm. Off exploring one day, I went into the barn and saw a rat disappearing into this hole. So I bundled up a pile of straw and lit it to see if I could catch sight of the rat again, but he was gone, so I dropped the straw and went off to explore somewhere else. I went to the beach to join the others, and when we all got back the barn was burned to the ground.

I told my da later that I did it, but at the time I kept my mouth shut.

That first trip outside the country with the Tenants' Association was to Benidorm, and I was nineteen. I know it was 1979 because coming home ours was the last flight permitted to land at Dublin Airport before they shut it down for the papal visit of John Paul II. As we waited to collect our luggage, hundreds of staff and officials were running around the airport like lunatics getting everything ready for him.

I remember sitting in the restaurant in Benidorm one day and the crowd I was with were all drinkers. I wasn't a drinker, so I said to Kathryn that I'd had enough and let's get the key to the place we were staying. The comedian Sil Fox was there telling jokes, though not in his day job as an entertainer; he lived in Finglas and was part of the whole trip. All the others seemed to be having a great time, but I had a pain in my hole. So Kathryn asked her da for the key, and the next thing there's this big row going on in the family. At the end of a lot of heated discussion, Kathryn's ma came over and gave us the key, explaining that her da didn't trust the mix of hot weather and youth – meaning he didn't trust me and Kathryn – so he was refusing to give us the key.

It was strange, but great, to be walking down to the shops in Benidorm and meeting half of your Finglas neighbours on the street. But what was stranger, especially coming from repressed Ireland, was all the drag queens. Benidorm is a big drag queen town and these were proper drag queens, not some big burly bloke with a wig and an Adam's apple. These looked like real beautiful women.

Two years later I left Ireland for my second holiday abroad. This time it was to Australia, and the land down under at the start of the 1980s was no place for drag queens, or any other man who didn't look manly enough. I'd got a big tax rebate and Kathryn had been saving hard. She was an apprentice hairdresser and she was on shit wages, around 4 pounds a week, when she started. But she would get tips, and she'd put her tips away and they would build and build. We left Ireland in February 1981. It was the day after the Valentine's night dance fire in the Stardust night club in Artane, Dublin. The fire killed forty-eight young people. I was reading about it in the papers when we were waiting to take off. A couple of mates of mine were in the Stardust that night but they survived, as did our bassist Tony's future wife.

Going from Ireland to Australia for a holiday was unheard of at the time. Kathryn had family out there who'd gone out some years before on the 6-pound boat fare subsidised by the Australian government. The Australian authorities were afraid of being overrun with Asians, so they were trying to attract white immigrants from our part of the world. With this in mind they made the fares to Australia very cheap, on condition that if you went back within less than two years you had to pay the full fare.

When we arrived in Australia it was with one eye on settling and making our lives there, like Kathryn's siblings had done. I saw the fantastic quality of life they had, and I was struck by the fact that they worked to live, whereas in Ireland people lived to work. They finished their day's work and then it was off to the beach or a barbeque by the pool. They have the climate for it, but they really do maximise their free time, and I loved that. Wherever I've gone in the world, I've always found that Irish people are successful because they have a great work ethic. I knew I had a really good work ethic too, so I thought I could do really well over there.

Australia had a lot to offer that really appealed to me. What didn't appeal to me, though, was the casual racism of a lot of Australians, especially towards the aboriginal people. It was very pervasive. And to see that – especially coming from Ireland where we've suffered a lot of oppression ourselves – it wasn't nice at all. This was almost forty years ago, and attitudes have changed, but I was getting abuse too for the way I looked. They'd be giving me ugly looks in the street and sneering 'faggot!' because my hair looked a bit weird to them.

In the end, the one thing that stopped me moving to Australia was the band, which had become Meelah XVIII by now, and in that endeavour Kathryn was 100 per cent behind me. When we got back from Australia we decided to get married. We saved for two years and tied the knot in 1983. Shortly after we got married I jacked in my Telecom job to go full time in music, which meant she was paying for everything. If we went out to the pictures or for a meal, she was paying. Everything we did, Kathryn was the one paying.

11

Stalking Depeche Mode

Bono called by the house when I was very ill and we got to talking about what inspires the songwriting process. He was asking why is it that we can't write a 'One' or a 'This Is' every time?

And I said to him, you know that fire you have within you when you're a youngster, a teenager, in your early twenties? Like, when we were in my first 'proper' band, Meelah XVIII, myself and the bass player Mick McKenna heard that Depeche Mode were coming to play in Dublin. Mick came from Basildon, in Essex, which was home to Depeche Mode, and he knew they used to hang out at this mall in the town at weekends. On the strength of this we got a boat to Holyhead, and a train down to London, and then went on the last twenty miles to Basildon by bus. We didn't have much of a plan; we just hung out at the shopping centre hoping to spot one of Depeche Mode so we could ask them for a support slot when they came to Dublin. Our entire plan basically boiled down to just blind hope, but that was the fire and the commitment we had at that age.

Of course, we never saw any of them at the shopping centre. They'd moved on from hanging around at malls to waiting for their call on *Top of the Pops*. We'd stayed with some relations of Mick's, and on the Monday morning we were heading back into London thinking, what a waste. Then, sitting there in front of us on the train is Andy Fletcher from the band. We can't fucking believe this! So we go up to him and tell him we've come all the way over from Ireland to ask for the support slot, and all he has to say in response to this massive effort we've made is that it has nothing to do with him and we'll have to ask the promoter.

We didn't get the support slot.

But the point was that when you're young you have that fire, that commitment. If there's even the slimmest thread of a chance of making something happen you go after it.

And Bono starts telling me similar stories about the first time himself and his girlfriend Ali went over to London, and they're getting the tube from record company to record company trying to get U2 demos heard.

Next minute Bono says, 'I'm working on this song,' and he jumps up and runs out to the car and comes back with his iPad and starts playing me this song. And here we are, two men in our fifties reminiscing in a kitchen, but that spark of enthusiasm from him right at that moment reminded me of when we were kids starting out in bands and you used to get that little buzz of creativity and you're trying to get the idea for a song down before it vanishes again. And it was very unpretentious and un-rock star-like.

And then the next day the TV news is on and I see he's having the First Lady of the United States, Michelle Obama, over for lunch . . .

12

Let's Get Serious

MEELAH XVIII, ST CANICE'S PARISH HALL, FINGLAS

I got there as Meelah XVIII were in full swing. What a great singer! 'Thinking Of You' was a bouncy Undertones-ish number with a catchy tune and obsessive chorus. 'Geriatrics' was a bit heavy on the drums, but overall Meelah XVIII can boast strong lyrics and an interesting sound. Their lead singer has a great vocal range and the kind of pubescent good looks that bring out the sexist in me.

Julie Parsons, 'Treasure on the Northside', *Hot Press*, 1982

We were starting to do our own gigs in places like The Magnet on Pearse Street, but one of our special homes was the Ivy Rooms on Parnell Street because it was beside where the No. 40 bus from Finglas stopped. This meant that all of our mates could go to the gig and get on the bus straight home afterwards with an almost door-to-door service. We used to jam the place, and I thought we were getting better as a band.

Then, one night, we were playing the upstairs part of the Ivy Rooms, which was the big part, and another Dublin band called Les Enfants were in the poky little space downstairs.

We had the main venue packed, and downstairs there were about ten people in the audience to see Les Enfants. This was a Saturday night. On Monday I opened the *Evening Herald* and there was this big splash saying, 'Les Enfants Sign Huge Record Deal'. And I'm looking at this story saying to myself, this lot can't even pull a crowd to that tiny place! I was dismayed.

Myself and Joe were still working for Telecom Eireann. Our keyboard player, Gerry Conlon, worked in the Guinness brewery, which was one of the best employers in Ireland. Our drummer had a decent job too. But at the next rehearsal I said to the others, 'Right, we're dropping the name Meelah XVIII and leaving our jobs.' I told them that the fact we had these jobs was robbing us of the hunger to succeed because the jobs were a safety net to fall back on. 'Let's chuck in the jobs. If there's no safety net we'll have to concentrate everything on the band.'

I've said earlier that there was no pressure from parents to get a job when there were no jobs, but it was a very different proposition when you already had a good job and you told your folks you wanted to give it up for music. I was newly married to Kathryn when I left Telecom Eireann to do music, but still my oul fella lost it because I was in a permanent and pensionable job. No one in their right mind gave up a permanent, pensionable job! He was still talking about it when I called in to see him just yesterday, all these years later. To this day he hasn't forgiven me for that!

Mick McKenna, the bassist, was still in school so it wasn't an issue for him, but the others wouldn't leave their jobs. So we were back to a three-piece of me, Joe and Mick. First up, we needed a new drummer. Alan Downey was in a local Finglas band called Alien Comfort. His da was a drummer and Alan had learned well. He was a good little drummer but he was younger than us and still at school – he had to get permission to play a lot of his early gigs with us because he was underage for being on licensed premises.

I went to see Alan and I told him we were getting this supergroup together and we wanted him on drums. He said to give him a week or two to think about it. I said, 'You cheeky little brat, I'm giving you the opportunity of a lifetime here!' But he kinda impressed me too with his cocky attitude. So Alan joined the band.

Tony McGuiness used to come to see Meelah XVIII all the time. Tony was born in London to Irish parents and only moved to Ireland in his early teens. He was a cousin of Steve Garvey, the bassist with one of the greatest punk bands, Buzzcocks. Tony was a cool fucker. He had the hair, and he was a huge Bowie fan, so I latched on to that. I told the others, 'I want him in the band, he looks great and he has great taste.' So we got Tony in on acoustic guitar.

You could get a little crap guitar and amp in Woolworths of Henry Street for about one-tenth of what you'd pay for a proper instrument in a music store, and that was the kind of shit we played. I went along to see U2 at the local school, Saint Bridget's, and here were these young kids with really expensive gear like a Gibson Flying V guitar and a Rickenbacker bass. We had nothing like that. The whole punk thing in Ireland was a bit of a farce – nice middle-class kids pretending to be hard cases coming from disadvantaged backgrounds.

But as soon as Tony joined, we knew that the first thing we needed to improve if we were going to go pro was our equipment. We handed him a banger of a guitar, and after one gig he said he was leaving the band.

'What?' I said. 'You can't leave. You've just joined.'

'I can't play with that guitar,' he replied. 'It's a heap of shit.'

So we went out and got him a decent, plastic, semi-acoustic Ovation and we started playing as a five piece – Joe, Mick, Alan, Tony and me. During breaks in rehearsals Tony would pick up Mick's bass and – *bippity-bop-bip-bip* – he'd put on this amazing show of slap bass-playing. Holy shit! Mick wasn't a bad bass player. Mick could play the bass, but Tony could *play* the bass. He could make it talk.

So we told Mick that he was on acoustic guitar from now on and Tony was on bass. But Mick wasn't having that, and rightly so when I think about it now. But Tony was just *so-o-o* good . . .

Mick left. Tony knew Billy McGuinness as a mate, while the rest of us would know Billy from around town as the frontman with bands like Free Booze and Blue Movies. We'd see Blue Movies in the Ivy Rooms and the band would be on stage doing their instrumental intro and Billy would be at the bar at the back of the venue. We'd all be looking at the band and then you'd hear this MC's voice booming out, filling the room: 'Billy will be on stage in twenty seconds!' And it was Billy at the back of the room with a radio mic giving himself the big build-up! Then he'd run the length of the place and jump on stage wearing this stupid bandana thing. And we'd be sitting there going, 'What a fucking wanker!' And he was. Having said all that, he was a real entertainer, and he really wanted to do backing vocals with us, so for a while Billy was semi-detached to the band.

It was time for a name change. At the start of the 1980s there were a load of bands with multi-word names like Orchestral Manoeuvres in the Dark, A Flock of Seagulls, Light A Big Fire, Cactus World News, Blue in Heaven and millions more, so we said, 'Let's do something concise, just one word.' We'd read *The Lion, the Witch and the Wardrobe* by C. S. Lewis, and in that book the Great White Witch stood for evil and Aslan was the force for good. Plus, we had a member of the band for each letter of the name. None of which matters, though it seemed to matter at the time.

13

And Then There Were Five

1983, LARK IN THE PARK, RAHENY, DUBLIN BAY

It was unbelievable. The music that was coming off the stage was amazing. They were unique. What I saw that day was a great band, but they didn't seem to know where their next gig was coming from. They hadn't been in contact with record companies or anything. I offered to become their manager.

Ex-manager Dick Fagan speaking in 1988

We had an outdoor gig coming up in St Anne's Park in Raheny, a Lark in the Park promoted by RTÉ Radio's *Dave Fanning Show*. For the occasion we got in a trio of backing vocalists, one of whom was Billy. Les Enfants – the band from the Ivy Rooms who'd spurred us to go full-time – were the headlining act and we were the openers, first on the bill.

Because we were the first band on, and because it was our biggest audience ever, we wanted to make an impact. I had a mate who was a stuntman. He'd recently worked on John Boorman's *Excalibur*, which was filmed in Wicklow with Helen Mirren, Liam Neeson and Gabriel Byrne. He said that he'd make sure we made an impact by setting himself on fire and running across the stage. We thought this would be brilliant, even if it wasn't really anything to do with the music. We were going to go with it, until the concert producer Ian Wilson got wind of it. He went ballistic at us! A fire hazard like that would blow the insurance cover for the whole gig. So when Ian knocked it on the head we had to fall back on Plan B.

The gig was set for a Sunday so, on the Friday before, we went to Ballyfermot industrial estate and bought blocks of dry ice. We were told to wrap the dry ice in layers of newspaper and put it in boxes to keep it airtight until the gig. After taking huge care to keep it airtight over the weekend, and to get it to the gig without it melting, we put our precious cargo into the dry ice machines that were to pump it out during our show. We thought dry ice was going to make it look like we were on *Top of the Pops*.

Puff! One gust of wind and our big special effect was gone. It was no more impressive than if someone had lit up a cigarette on stage.

Despite the dry ice disaster, we must have made some impression because after we came off stage the event's MC Dave Fanning asked us to do a recording session for his show on RTÉ Radio 2. The Fanning Sessions were an Irish version of the Peel Sessions on BBC Radio, where John Peel gave a break to hundreds of acts including The Undertones and Joy Division. The very first band to record a Fanning Session were U2 four years earlier, and now they were filling stadiums everywhere on their 'War' world tour. To get an invite to record a Fanning Session was a sign that you'd arrived, and that you might be casting off again very soon for bigger things.

Shortly afterwards, we turned up in the Montrose studios of RTÉ, recorded three songs in a rush, and they were rubbish. What we did get from the session was 190 pounds, and it was the first time we'd ever earned money, because you'd always lose money from gigs. Between paying for the hire of the PA system and a van to transport the gear, you'd always be out of pocket. Your dole payment would subsidise your gigs.

We went straight from recording the session to the Boot Inn at the back of Dublin Airport, cashed the RTÉ cheque and got twisted. At that time we were rehearsing in Alan's folks' garage from nine til five on weekdays. It must have been an absolute nightmare for the neighbours, the noise we were making. Billy would come up to Alan's garage around two or three every afternoon when he'd finished his shift in Boland's Bakery. He'd always arrive with a load of cakes, and that's the only reason we'd let him join in with us – for the cakes.

But this particular day, the day after blowing our big cheque at the Boot Inn, Billy arrived up at Alan's garage at nine in the morning.

'What are *you* doing here?' we asked him.

'Yez asked me to join last night!'

Aw, no-o-o ...

'Jeez, Billy, we didn't mean it. We were locked last night. We were all in a good humour.'

But Billy had quit his job that morning, and that's how he got into the band.

Not long after Billy joined we had to find somewhere else to rehearse, because we were there making noise six days a week and the neighbours couldn't take it anymore. We came in contact with Eoin O'Hagan whose family had a farm with a pigsty they weren't using. The pigsty had nine-inch solid walls with a corrugated iron roof, and it used to get freezing in the winter. We had a blanket to wrap up the drums for transporting them, and I used to wrap myself in the blanket with just the top of the mic sticking out, because if I took my hands out of the blanket they'd stick to the mic.

It was a great place to rehearse though, because the noise wasn't disturbing anyone. It had other attractions too. The airline people used to use the spot outside the pigsty to train the air-hostesses in emergency drills like how to put out fires. We'd take a break from playing to watch them being put through their paces, like a spectator sport.

14

This Is It! Oh No it's Not, Says Bono!

There was a generic sound coming from all these Dublin bands at the time, partly because a lot of bands seemed to be just different combinations of the same people. You'd see such-and-such a person playing guitar with a band on Tuesday, and the next night he'd be playing bass with another band. They all drank in poseur pubs around Grafton Street like Bruxelles and The Bailey, and that lent itself to this generic groupthink sound of the city.

I didn't want to have anything to do with that, and because we came from Finglas and Ballymun we wouldn't have been accepted into that clique anyway. So we locked ourselves in the pigsty for a year and that's where we wrote and wrote and wrote. One of our strongest new songs was 'Breaking Up', and everyone kept saying we should release it as our first single. I said no, that's not it yet. Then we wrote 'This Is' and I just knew, *this is it*, this is the one.

Everyone in the band was trying to outdo the others, trying to be the cleverest. I was trying to pack the most high notes and most low notes into the singing, while Joe wanted the best solos and Tony wanted all these fretless basslines sliding all over the place. I remember reading an interview with Sting around that time where he said that when he started out he made the mistake of trying to get the kitchen sink into every song, but that as he matured he came to realise that less is more. And a lot of the feedback from the record companies early on had been just that – that the songs were too long and rambling and not concise enough. So we decided to take this philosophy on board and strip the songs down and make them more compact.

In the case of 'This Is', it started out as a really fast song with a totally different chorus, which I thought was shit, so we shelved it. Then one day we'd run out of songs to rehearse and we pulled it off the shelf and said, 'Let's see what we can do with this.' Other band members have said that the start of 'This Is' was inspired by 'Drive' by The Cars, and maybe that is the case. I can't recall exactly. We slowed down the manic pace and it sounded better, but we still hadn't got a chorus for it. I loved 'There Must Be An Angel' by Eurythmics and the way Annie Lennox was going up and down the octaves – before the likes of Mariah Carey and Whitney Houston started making shite of that technique.

Around the time that 'This Is' was coming together as a showpiece song, our live shows were starting to attract the attention of the English A&R pack. CBS were the first label to show an interest in us, to the point that we got down to serious talking. Every little detail in the contract took ages. For instance, our Irish identity was important to us, so we wanted it stated in the contract that we'd record the first Aslan album in Dublin. We'd ring the CBS Dublin office and they'd ring CBS London, and a week later London would ring back, and this was going on for every little detail! So this dragged on and on and on and on for six or seven months, until one day I got a pain in my bollix with it and I dragged all the lads into my Escort and drove over to the CBS offices in the city. We turned up unannounced, and the people there were flustered. We were told the head of the Irish operation was in a meeting and would we like to come back later. We said we'd wait. We sat in the hallway and waited, and waited, and eventually the top man came out.

'Right,' I said, 'we've a pain in the bollix with this. Are you signing us or are you not signing us?'

'Well, no,' he said. 'We're not.'

'What!?'

Here I am trying to force their hand and it's backfired!

It hadn't backfired, of course. Our appearance there had just brought things to a head quicker because at that stage they'd made the decision they weren't going to sign us anyway. I remember driving us all back to the pigsty that day. I was driving through Drumcondra and I swear to God I thought about crashing the car into a bleedin' wall. I'll never forget the rage that filled me for that millisecond. I wanted to turn the wheel and just ram the car into a wall. Seven months gone down the drain. And making it worse was that, as far as the band were concerned, throughout that seven months we were signed all that time – we were just hammering out the final small details.

But that wasn't the end of it. Now, because CBS had rejected us, nobody else would touch us. Ensign, Chrysalis, all the others that had shown a bit of interest – *whoosh!* – they all flew away. There would be more lost time before a major label would show any interest again.

With CBS pulling out and scaring off the rest of them, we had to go away for another six months, back to the pigsty. It was like going into quarantine. We kept our heads down, rehearsed hard, and came out once in a while to play The Danceline club. The Danceline on North Great George's Street was big but still intimate enough to build a great atmosphere. Steady Eddie and Pete the Roz ran the show. Those gigs were great for us because they let us show people what a great live band we had become during our period of enforced decontamination.

Our first recording of 'This Is' was rough and ready, but I knew without doubt that it was good. So I thought straight-away, Mother Records. They've been set up by Bono to help young bands who've been shafted by the business. Let's take it to them.

Myself and Joe arranged to meet Bono in the Dockers pub on the quays. He arrives two hours late, orders a sausage sandwich and tells us, 'Yeah, I've had a listen to it and it's not great. But I'll arrange to give you a recording machine, and you can tape your whole set and I'll pick out a song.' I was disgusted. I said to myself, bollix to that – 'This Is' is a great song.

For years I carried that resentment against Bono because I thought we epitomised everything that Mother Records stood for, or should have stood for. We were a young band. We'd been shafted by every record company in the business. We were on the way up but still looking for a leg-up. We were all the things that Mother purported to be there for.

In reality, at the time it wasn't a fit, so it didn't happen. I got over it. Looking back now at the logistics of it, it wasn't as simple as I thought at the time. But I got paranoid to the point that I became very suspicious of Mother Records.

In my mistrustful state of mind I got to thinking: Mother Records have access to every new idea that's germinating in Irish music, because every band in Ireland with a fresh idea puts it on a tape and sends it into Mother. There's U2 with access to all these fresh new ideas, so maybe it's a good thing that we're not signing to Mother. I eventually came to realise that those suspicions were just my paranoia at the time. Great conspiracy theory though, isn't it!

I remember reading Bono in a lot of his early interviews and thinking that he did a lot of talking but not a lot of saying. You'd read a really long interview in, say, *Hot Press*, and he'd drag you into the interview but then you'd get to the end and think – what did he actually say there?

It was the same that day we met him at the Dockers.

I couldn't wait to get back to tell the rest of the band we'd had this meeting with Bono. The others were waiting on tenterhooks back at the pigsty. Myself and Joe flew back, got in, and they all wanted to know: 'How did it go?'

I started to tell them, 'Well, he said . . .'

But before I could go any further I was asking myself, what *did* Bono say?

I was so caught up in the moment, and the whole buzz of meeting him and pitching our songs, that it was only now, facing the others, that I realised he'd told us to fuck off. He didn't say 'fuck off', but that was the message. He told us to ring his office on Monday and they'd give us a lend of this eight-track recorder. He said 'This Is' didn't have a chorus, and maybe we had some better songs. He said all that, but without sounding like he was saying it.

The first time I ever heard Bono say anything where I thought, *Bang!* Yeah, you have it there, was his story of the burning car. It's America, and there's a kid at the bottom of the hill looking up at a man at the top of the hill with his big car. The kid says, 'Some day I'll drive a car like that, I'll have a house like that and I'll live like that.' In Ireland the kid looks up to the top of the hill and he says, 'I'm going to burn that car the minute he goes out the door.'

I thought, you've got that bang on, Bono.

15

Rugby Tickets and Cocaine

It's all psychological warfare. It really wears you down and affects your nerves. I was being supported by my wife at this stage and the lads in the band were permanently broke. One Tuesday I remember coming out of the labour after picking up the dole and going straight down to the Gresham Hotel for lunch with some record company executives. We had a solicitor in London, an accountant in Dublin, yet there wasn't one of us that could afford to buy a cup of coffee.

Dick Fagan speaking in 1988

The first time we played The Danceline we supported Toy With Rhythm, who were doing a showcase. They were being managed by this flash English guy called Danny Kenny.

Shortly after the gig I did an interview with *In Dublin* magazine. I wasn't used to doing interviews so I didn't know that there are things you should and shouldn't say, and I just stated the plain fact that we got a better response from the audience than Toy With Rhythm. It was just an off-the-cuff remark. A week later I was in the little cafe at Litton Lane Studios, having lunch after rehearsing, and Danny Kenny comes up to our table and says in his cocky English accent, 'You little cunt. What have you been saying about my fucking band?'

And I'm thinking, who is this little English prick? So my response was, 'Who do you think you are? And now fuck off!'

I don't know what it was but something clicked. Probably that we'd stood up for ourselves. He came back to us soon after and said himself and his partner John Reid wanted to manage us.

At the time Dick Fagan was negotiating for us. We had put the CBS letdown behind us, and we'd done our time in quarantine when no other label would touch us. The whole country was crawling with A&R men and we were using it to our advantage. All these record companies would be having a look at you, and if they had any interest they'd usually give you a grand and send you into a studio to record a demo for them. Then, when the demo was recorded, they'd have a two-day first refusal on it. After that you could hawk it around. So we were getting studio experience and songs demoed at the expense of the record companies. That's how 'This Is' came about. I can't remember which company it was because there were so many at the time, but some label gave us 1,000 pounds and we used it to record four songs in Litton Lane Studios, and 'This Is' was one of them.

Some little bits of good came out of this manic period, but that whole time was a nightmare because the record labels would court you, and they'd bring you out for meals, they'd bring you right to the edge of it, telling you you're signed, and then you wouldn't hear another word from them.

We did one session in Litton Lane Studios for Ensign Records. We were in one room and Sinéad O'Connor was in the other. Ensign had a load of acts recording demo material in adjoining studios at that time, but we were the ones they were really over to see on that trip. Sinéad was just some young wan who'd come along by-the-by, but when it was over she was the one that got signed. So there's all this stuff happening around you and you don't know whether you're up or you're down.

A lot of the record company A&R men were cunts. They didn't give a fuck what band they were looking at. A lot of the time they didn't even *know* what band they were looking at. As far as most of them were concerned, they were on a junket over to Dublin, and Dublin at that time was a very happening place. You had Def Leppard and Frankie Goes to Hollywood and Spandau Ballet and all these acts over doing the tax haven thing, and there was a real buzz about town. So these record company A&R heads would ring ahead from London and say, 'Ireland are playing England in the rugby, so will you get us tickets?' And then, when they arrive, they're sending you around the place looking for cocaine for them. We did get them the rugby tickets.

We quickly sussed what was going on, how we were being used, and that's when we decided that we were going to use it to our advantage. If they wanted tickets and coke from us, we told them we wanted money from them to demo songs. It wasn't so much that we wanted to demo songs to play to people, more that we wanted to get them into the studio to find out what was wrong with them. It was a learning curve for us in the studio.

Having said that, while we tried to make the best of it as

a trade-off, in our hearts we knew it was a piss-poor trade-off because what we wanted was a record deal. At that time the be-all and end-all of your existence was to be signed. Probably no Irish band could see any further than getting their signature on that contract, and we were as guilty as anyone else on that count. It was only when we got signed that we realised this was only the beginning of everything – that being signed in itself meant fuck all.

16

Close to Killing Each Other

Record company people are really sheep. If one seems interested they all want in on the act. Muff Winwood, who's God
in the A&R business, really liked the band, so all of a sudden
all the record companies were contacting me. There were
people from America ringing me in the middle of the night.
At one gig in the TV Club we had fifteen people over, competing to sign the band, including publishing executives and
A&R men. I had to hire a mini-bus to drive them all around.

Dick Fagan speaking in 1988

We put on a showcase at the Television Club on a Saturday
afternoon. The Television Club on Harcourt Street was a
huge place, but on this strange afternoon there was only a
group of record company A&R men and our manager, Dick,
making up the audience, while we thundered through an
entire set as if we were playing to a full crowd. Trying to fake
that intensity was hard work.

At the end of our performance everything looked great.
The people from Chrysalis Records told us they wanted to
sign the band. That was it! Welcome to the Promised Land.
They just had to work out the economics of it. Chrysalis
already had our future mapped out in such detail that first

up they were going to put us on this radical new TV show called *Max Headroom* hosted by a stuttering android. We were going to be a pioneering act. 'We'll iron out the details on Monday, but the deal is there. You're signed. End of story.' We celebrated. We couldn't tell anybody, but we knew within ourselves that we'd done it!

A couple of days later, I'm at home on the Monday morning of the big day when Aslan are supposed to officially become a Chrysalis Records act. Around eight o'clock I get a phone call and it's Dick. He's in Dublin Airport and he's supposed to be flying out to London to seal the deal. He tells me that he can't do this, the pressure's too much. There's panic and shouting and screaming at both ends of the phone line, but in the end he doesn't go.

So that's how the Chrysalis thing hit the wall, and that's how we ended up with no manager. I'm not sure that his failure to show up in London that day is why the deal fell through. Chrysalis had already signed Les Enfants. It could be they decided they already had one Irish band and didn't need another. You don't know, but it had all fallen apart again and we were on our knees.

With Dick gone, Danny Kenny and John Reid stepped into the management role. They'd gotten Cactus World News a deal with MCA, so we thought, okay, they know the formula.

Up to the arrival of Danny Kenny we were getting all this interest from record companies, but we had no one running the show that knew how to play one off against the other. When Danny and John Reid came on board that all changed.

They took that side of it out of our hands so we could concentrate on getting the music right.

That was the case for a while, but then the pair of them had a falling out, and one day we get a call from Danny and he says, 'Right, lads, me and John are splitting up. It's make-your-mind-up time. You're either going with John or you're going with me.'

It seemed a clear choice. John was always the one who would stay in the background and say nothing. Danny would be doing all the talking. He was the one with all the sparkle. So we had a talk among ourselves and decided we'd go with Danny because he seemed to be the one doing the business.

John Reid today in 2019 is President of Live Nation Europe Concerts, having been President of Warner Music Europe. John works with acts like Madonna, Michael Bublé and the Red Hot Chili Peppers. He's one of the most successful music business figures in the world. We picked the other one of course.

To be fair to Danny, the first thing he did was to pull us back from courting all these record companies and send us back to basics, which meant back to the pigsty at Dublin Airport. He said, 'Go back to the pigsty, get back to writing, finish this album.'

And that's what we did. We went back to the pigsty with two or three songs complete, and we came out with all the songs written for our debut album, *Feel No Shame*. Disappearing off this time wasn't like the last time, when it felt like we'd been sent into exile as a punishment. We came back a fresh prospect. That's not to say that shutting ourselves away like that was a holiday. Frustrations would boil over from time to time. There was one violent explosion over something as stupid as a bridge between two songs. To begin with the two songs joined up. The end of one ran into the start of the other, and I thought that worked well, but the others decided to split the two. This meant they had to write an end to one and a beginning for the other. They were spending the day doing that.

So they're working on instrumental arrangements and I'm sitting there in this shed built of breeze blocks and a corrugated steel roof in the middle of a field in the middle of winter and I'm absolutely petrified with the cold. They had a Superser heater beside them down the end where they were playing their instruments. I had nothing. As I've mentioned before, there was a blanket we used to wrap around the drums for transport, so I wrapped that around me for warmth while I waited for them to finish.

They finally finished, and they played the new arrangements for me and asked me what I thought. From the outset I didn't think it was a good idea to separate the songs, and I thought the new arrangements did nothing for them, so I told them it sounded shite. At that, Tony drags me out of my blanket and starts kicking me around the place. It was a serious battering. There was blood coming out of me. His vibe was that they'd been working on this all day and I'd been sitting on my arse all day, which was true, but that's the way the process was by design. It had to be that way because I didn't play an instrument. And I honestly thought what they came up with was shit. It didn't work, and that's all I was saying, but he was so pissed off. I think he was taking his frustration out on me because he knew it wasn't working after spending a whole day on it.

It turned nasty but we didn't hold grudges. If we had a problem we'd get it out of our systems. Even though that particular case of musical differences turned into a bit of a fight, it got it out of our systems. I came to practice the next day and just carried on as usual. It wasn't a big deal. You got the hiding and then argued it out after, and by the end of the day it was over. It was like when brothers fight – when it's over it's over and you just carry on with life in the family as normal.

That wasn't a typical incident. That was kinda heavy, but there were other times when things boiled over. We were living in each other's pockets. We were stuck together every day rehearsing in an isolated pigsty, detached from contact with other people. Touring was worse because you were all squeezed together in the confined space of a little van, with all the gear. There was one time, some years later, when we were heading down the country in a splitter bus. Splitters are vans customised to cram band members and equipment into a tiny space at the highest possible density, like a really uncomfortable game of Tetris. Billy was driving, and I made a joke about his mot, his woman.

He slams on the brakes and jumps out and pulls back the sliding side door. And I was only joking but he's standing there: 'Get out! Get out!'

I told him, 'I'm not getting out. I'm only joking. She's a

lovely girl.' I wouldn't get out. He was raging. He was really going to do me damage. There was a lot of that sort of stuff going on.

By its very nature, touring brings out the worst in people. Personal tics get to be big issues. Suppose someone in the band sucks their teeth – *psssstp, psssstp* – and you're sitting stuck in a van beside someone going *psssstp, psssstp* for five hours all the way down to Dingle, and then for five hours all the way home in the middle of the night. You want to fucking kill them. Or if someone clicks their knuckles the whole time and they're not even aware they're doing it. It would drive you mental.

That's why we'd do mad things on the road. On one trip we got a pile of high-pressure water pistols. We'd pull up at a bus stop and jump out with these pistols and people would be diving for cover, thinking we were going to really shoot them. This was the time of the Troubles, when people really were getting gunned down in the street. We wouldn't be thinking of how these people at the bus stop felt – that they might genuinely be in fear of their lives – all that mattered was to burst the monotony of being together, because when you're confined together like that it's very intense.

We'd play card games for forfeits. Switch was the game we'd play most and whoever lost had to do a forfeit at the end of the day. One that I was landed with was to walk into a shop and ask for a pack of cigarettes, and when the woman asked for payment I had to tell her, 'I'm Christy Dignam. I don't pay for cigarettes.' The rules were that I couldn't break down laughing and tell her it was only a joke. I had to walk out serious and straight-faced without paying.

Another time Joe had to crawl through the busy town centre of Portlaoise on all fours, dragged along by Alan on a dog lead. A lot of people stopped and stared. These are the things you do to stop yourselves killing each other on the road, and there were times we did come close to killing each other.

17

So Phillo, What's it Like to Be Famous?

By the close of 1985, we needed to do something, anything, to get some momentum up again. I went to Jim Butler of Reekus Records, a little independent label, to try to convince him to put out 'This Is' as a single. I played Jim our demo of the song and he loved it. He said to leave it with him overnight and he'd play it for Elvera Butler, who was his partner at the time. So I said, 'No, if you want to hear it tomorrow I'll come back in tomorrow and play it for Elvera. I'm not having you sitting here ripping it apart and finding every fault with it.' Jim looked at me as if I was mad, but he rang me that night and said, 'I think we're going to go with this. Come in tomorrow and we'll play it for Elvera.'

I arrived the next day and there's Phil Lynott sitting in reception, waiting to go into a meeting. I nearly shat myself. To me, Phil epitomised the Rock Star. He had that glint in the eye. He had the rock star coolness. He had everyone eating out of his hand. He had it all. And then there was the drugs thing. I bought into all that. That to me was what a rock star was and did. It was the same with Keith Richards. He was how a rock star looked and behaved.

Years later I would come to resent the likes of Lou Reed and all these people who endorsed heroin chic. They had a huge responsibility for where that went, for making it seem cool and desirable. They seemed like gods, but in the end they were only humans, and they fucked up. People like Lou Reed were riding the first wave of heroin, when American soldiers were bringing it back from Vietnam, so they wouldn't have known where it would lead.

Myself and Phillo get talking, and I say to him, 'I know this might sound stupid, but what's it like to be a rock star?'

It was a grey, overcast, rainy day in Dublin. Phil looks at me and says, 'I'll tell you what it's like ... today anyone can walk from here, the length of Grafton Street to O'Connell Bridge, wearing a pair of sunglasses and nobody will bat an eyelid. But you have a hit single and do that and they'll all be glaring at that rock star prick – who does he think he is? It's not you that changes,' Phil tells me. 'It's other people's attitudes that change.'

I didn't understand what he meant at the time. I'd no concept. But he was 1,000 per cent right. That's the way it is.

In Ireland people – especially people who are parochial, in the sense that they grew up close to you – believe they're entitled to come up to you and tell you, 'Christy, you're a wanker. What you should have done was this ...' They have the whole detailed plan for how you should have lived your life and how you should be living your life. They're telling me that I'd be living in a mansion on Killiney Hill right now if I'd just stuck to their plan. And the nearer you are to the place where you grew up, the more entitled people feel to give you that advice.

Within a short time of us chatting, Phil was dead. I wanted to have an association with him, and when we were doing 'Feel No Shame' we asked for and got Tim Martin to engineer, who had been Phil's engineer. Tim gave me a jacket that had belonged to Phil. When you opened it, it had all these stickers for stuff like Thin Lizzy at the Hammersmith Odeon. It got robbed out of my car, and whoever robbed it didn't even know what it was. It was just another leather jacket.

Jim and Elvera at Reekus agreed to release 'This Is' as a vinyl single. As far as I'm concerned, that rough version recorded with Chris O'Brien in a four-track studio is far better than the one we later recorded for the album with the best studio facilities EMI's money could buy. We only pressed 1,000 vinyl copies, but it transformed our fortunes.

18

The Day it All Came Good

This is, quite simply, the best Irish single I've heard all year.
It has everything – a great tune, even better lyrics, and a
passionate delivery. Christy Dignam's singing is so soulful
and intense it's impossible not to be moved by it.

Radio DJ Mark Cagney reviews 'This Is', 1986

We had a single that was blaring out of the radio wherever
we went but we were still playing to audiences of 200 people
in the Baggot Inn. Then, while the single was still riding high
in the charts, we supported Cactus World News at another
open-air festival under the Lark in the Park banner. This one
was the Lark by the Lee in Cork. It took place on a scorching
summer's day during the 1986 World Cup Finals in Mexico.
In fact, it was the day that Diego Maradona scored against
England with the 'Hand of God' and followed up with one
of the greatest goals ever seen.

When we went on stage in Cork that day, there were 15,000
people there on a Sunday lunchtime, and they were there for
us. I can still remember how gratifying that felt. We'd put in
years of blood, sweat and tears, and finally, on that day, it
all came good. When we came off the stage drenched with

sweat we were agreed that if it all ended there and then – if that was the end of the band – we would all have gone home happy saying everything we'd gone through was worth it.

The drinks company Beamish & Crawford was sponsoring the event, and after the show we all went back to the brewery for a party. We got wasted to the point that Alan and Billy fell asleep in the van on the way home. So we stripped the pair of them naked and gaffer-taped Billy's hand around Alan's dick, and vice versa. Then we woke them up. There was blue murder!

At the end of the year *Hot Press* held its annual poll where the readers got to vote in various categories. They listed the top three vote-getters for Irish Single of the Year. One was 'In A Lifetime' by Clannad and Bono. One was something by Christy Moore. And beating them all for Single of the Year was 'This Is' by Aslan. As far as we were concerned that was a piece of poetic justice, because it wasn't as if we'd gone into Windmill Lane with the bare bones of that song and got a producer in to make something of it. It was the *exact* same demo that we'd given Bono, which he'd said wasn't good enough because it had 'no chorus'.

Many years after it first hit the charts, we got confirmation that 'This Is' really is a good song with a timeless quality. A very famous pop Svengali came to us and said he wanted 'This Is' and 'Crazy World' for two of his international chart-topping acts. But there was one major condition attached: we had to pretend that one of the Svengali's stable of stars co-wrote 'This Is' with the band, which meant this performer we'd never met would get 50 per cent of the royalties. I pointed out that everyone in Ireland knows that we wrote 'This Is' and that the other individual had nothing to do with it. In fact, the individual in question was probably still in short trousers when the song was a huge hit the first time around.

His exact words were: 'Yeah, well I don't give a fuck about Ireland.'

He told us that Aslan had earned all we were ever going to earn from 'This Is', but if we signed it away to him we could look forward to earning vast amounts of money from a worldwide hit.

I said, 'Yeah, but we'd have to say that your sidekick wrote our song, and we can't do that.'

19

Limos, Doctors, Everything on Tap

FEBRUARY 1987, ST PATRICK'S COLLEGE, DRUMCONDRA

The predominantly female audience responds as if Aslan have stepped straight off the pages of *Smash Hits* instead of the 36a bus. Two encores to finish, then they're joined in their dressing room by Janice Long – who has repeated their session on her BBC Radio 1 programme three times – and a collection of men with English accents and tour jackets. The band chat amiably with Janice but there's a noticeable proliferation of forced smiles and strained banter when the A&R men compliment them on a fine set.

George Byrne, *Hot Press*

Around this time Janice Long was presenting *Top of the Pops* every second week, but she was also getting into John Peel territory, looking for new talent to put on her BBC radio show. We were playing all the toilets around England and she was going to a lot of those type of gigs. All these years later she's still doing her sessions, and we did one for her in Northern Ireland very recently.

By the spring of 1987 we were finally starting to take off. We played 'Loving Me Lately' at the televised Irish Music

Awards in the National Concert Hall. One hour later we were due onstage at the Olympic Ballroom off Camden Street. You could walk from one venue to the other in three minutes, but Danny Kenny hired a limo to take us the few hundred yards in rock star style. That night Danny told us, 'Welcome to your new life!', even though we were still on the dole. Were we delighted to go along with all this pampered star-tripping? Of course we were! We got to the venue and the place was jammed with 2,000 people. But just before we were to go on stage we had a dressing-room emergency when one of us had a panic attack and it looked like we might have to cancel.

A phone call was put out to this music biz doctor who was always on call if anything went wrong. I'd gone to him one time with pleurisy and he crushed this vial on his desk and told me to snort it because it would get into my system quicker that way. The music biz doctor arrived, we got through our crisis, and we played one of the gigs of our lives.

That's how it was now. Limousines, doctors if you needed them, everything on tap. If you had a problem it was sorted and we were blinded by that. At the time we thought it was about having a few joints and a few beers. We never did coke up until then. This brought things to a whole other level.

I remember the trauma of just trying to score a little bit of hash only a few years earlier. One place you could be pretty sure of getting it was a poky pub on Dorset Street. I went in the first time and made discreet enquiries. I was told: 'The man with the red hair there, sitting at the bar. He's the one selling it.'

So I'm sitting there for half an hour while the bloke on the barstool is chatting with the barman. I'm waiting for the barman to move, but the place is very quiet and he just stays there and chats. After I've waited about forty-five minutes, the barman finally walks away to serve someone else. So I fly over to the bloke on the stool.

'Can I get a ten-spot?'

He looks at me and shouts down to the barman, 'Pat!' The barman comes over and right now I don't know what I've gotten myself into. Is this a set-up? Then the barman pulls out a bag of ten-spots wrapped in tinfoil from under the counter.

I handed over my tenner, looked at this skinny ten-spot and thought, what a rip. That was around the time that the whole hash thing went out of the hippies' hands and into the hands of the criminal gangs. When I first started out, I could count on the fingers of one hand the amount of people in Finglas who smoked hash, and they were all hippies. Then serious criminal gangs like the Dunnes started to get into it.

Danny brought us to the likes of the Pink Elephant, which were as far from the dive on Dorset Street as you could get. We'd never been in the Pink Elephant. We'd never wanted to be in the Pink Elephant. We weren't part of that shit. We were opposed to all that. After poseur pubs like The Bailey and Bruxelles stopped serving, all the groupthink musicians went to the Pink for late drinks. We were against all that but Danny told us, 'No, you have to be seen in these places. This is where Def Leppard and Frankie Goes to Hollywood hang out.' That was enough reason for us, and we were sucked in, and once you're sucked into it you're enjoying it because it *is* an enticing life – at the time you're living it.

With the flash nightclubs came the coke. There was a bloke who's passed away now called the Elder Lemon. He used to make flight cases for band instruments upstairs in Litton Lane Studios. The Elder Lemon went over to Colombia and bought a kilo of cocaine. He flew from the Colombian capital Bogotá to Paris, timing his journey to arrive in Paris for a rugby match there between Ireland and France. He flew into Dublin with all the returning rugby fans, carrying this large amount of pure cocaine. On odd occasions some of that coke would make its way to the band as a reward for achieving something, or if there was something to celebrate. And that was something we got accustomed to.

Then we went over to America and we got more intense with the coke, because it was laid on for us. We came back to Ireland and the others got back to business as usual, but I couldn't stop because I'm an addict and I had to keep going. I'd been messing with heroin before I went over, and when I came back I couldn't get a lot of coke so I started doing a bit of gear.

20

Occupation Rock Star

It was the spring of 1987 and we were in the EMI building in Manchester Square being brought up through the floors, where each level we passed was plusher than the previous one. We got to the boardroom on the top floor and we were signing the contracts and the champagne corks were popping, and I remember sitting there thinking something's not right. All the pressure of the past few years had been about this big drive to get signed. I thought that when we signed there'd be some great feeling of fulfilment, of achievement, and then we actually signed and I remember sitting back, and Billy was saying he's keeping the cork from this champagne bottle as a memento of this great occasion, and I'm looking at him thinking ... thinking that at this great moment I felt nothing. I just felt nothing. It was really weird, after all the build-up, nothing. Here we were signing to one of the biggest record labels in the world – we were now on the same label as our hero David Bowie – and I just felt poxy, really unfulfilled. Instead of being in the moment, I just kept thinking ahead to all this work we now had in front of us.

After we got back to Ireland I went to the dole office to collect my labour as usual. I was trying to drag out signing off, and I was hoping to keep collecting for another few weeks at least. But I was about to pay the price of our new fame and, when I got to the top of the line, yer man behind the counter says, 'Aren't you part of that band Aslan? I've seen the posters up.'

So I had to tell him the purpose of my visit was to sign off the labour. When Tony signed off there was a space on the form asking what his new occupation was going to be. Tony wrote: 'Rock star'.

I felt no sense of achievement or fulfilment when we finally signed that deal we'd craved for so long, but the birth of my daughter, Kiera, was nothing but achievement, fulfilment and love. I was with Kathryn for the birth in the Rotunda Hospital, when the doctor started screaming that the baby was going into distress, and the heartbeat of the baby was dropping. I was terrified! With most people you fall in love with, you meet them and then fall in love with them over a period of time. But I hadn't met Kiera. She was just a lump in Kathryn's stomach. I didn't know her. She didn't have an identity. But when she was struggling to be born, I was filled with this urge to protect her. I'd have died for her or killed for her. She was purple when she came out because she'd been in stress. It was terrifying, but when she was okay it was an amazing feeling. It was probably the best feeling I've ever had in my life. For love to hit me that quickly, I was bowled over. It was one of the most profound experiences I've ever had.

21

A Dangerous Secret

The first time I got stoned on heroin I didn't feel, wow, I'm on a different plane! I'd taken hash, it was nice. I'd had drink, it was nice. I took coke, it was nice. But when I took heroin for the first time I just felt I was home. I thought, this is how Johnny wakes up in the morning, this is how Mary wakes up in the morning, this is how everyone wakes up in the morning; but this is how I should feel waking up in the morning. I felt whole for the first time in my life.

It's like all your life you've been hungry and you have that gnawing emptiness inside you, and for the very first time that hunger is gone. I'd always been vaguely aware of this emptiness. It had always made me feel distant from everyone and everything in my life, even my family and the people closest to me. Heroin just closed up or filled in that distance.

So you wake up the next day after taking it and you have a choice. You can either go with this hole that you've had all your life, or ...

I first took heroin in the early 1980s when it was only coming into this country for the first time. I was nineteen or twenty. There were no addicts hanging out on the streets of Dublin looking like skeletons to scare me off it. We'd all seen the heroin addicts on *Kojak*, slumped in a filthy alleyway banging up, needles in their arms, but that TV fantasy stuff seemed to have nothing to do with the reality in Dublin. I came across it for the first time when I went to score some hash from this Hell's Angel in the Mount Pleasant flats on Dublin's south side. The biker was asleep and his girlfriend told me there was no hash, only skag. I had no idea what skag was, but I wasn't going to show my ignorance so I said I'd take a ten-spot.

A ten-spot of hash those days might be the size of your little finger, but here I am looking at this tiny bit of powder she's handed me thinking I've wasted my money. I had to ask her what to do with it.

'Just snort it. It's a lovely buzz.'

It happened to be my younger brother's birthday that weekend, so a load of us piled into a couple of cars and drove out to the beach at Donabate, north of the city, for a party. It was going to be an all-nighter with loads of drink and a barbeque, but we drove around the dunes for ages trying to find a sheltered spot that was flat enough to pitch our tents. It was nearly dark by the time we found this nice flat patch of grass.

So we cooked some burgers, drank loads of wine and smoked loads of hash, and I started thinking about the little bag of skag in my pocket. By now I'd worked out that this was heroin, but I knew not to say anything to anyone. I knew this thing was taboo, and at the same time I'm looking at this speck of powder thinking, this can't do anything, what a waste of money. I snorted it and straight away I felt it.

I was lying down on the grass, looking into the dancing

flames of the fire and out over the glistening sea. I felt warm and safe. I felt that I was just right. People have this idea of being 'high' on drugs, but this wasn't a high. I just thought to myself, *This is what you're supposed to feel like when you wake up in the morning.*

When I did wake up the next morning, I didn't have time to work out how I felt. My brother stuck his head into my tent in a bit of a panic and told me to get out quick and see what we'd done. We'd pitched our tents in the dark on the green of a golf course. The place was trashed, between the bottles, and bits of burgers and the remains of the fire we'd built. There were golfers standing there staring at this scene and they were not happy. We legged it back to Finglas in a hurry.

But even on the drive back I was thinking about how I'd woken up the morning after taking heroin and everything was okay. I wasn't dead. I wasn't filled with this craving to rush out looking for more. I was thinking that if someone had said to me on that drive home, 'That's it, the world has run out of heroin', I'd have said, grand, no problem. And it was years later before I did do it again. I renewed my acquaintance with it when I came in contact with this bloke working in an industrial estate near me. He'd have a smoke at lunchtimes at the back of the factory, so I started calling to him on his lunch breaks and we'd both smoke some gear. Then I started buying a tiny bit off him for the odd Saturday night, and that became every Saturday. Then I started getting enough so that I'd have a small bit left over for Sunday. Then I'd buy enough so I'd be able to stretch it into Monday.

This all happened very gradually, maybe over two years,

so I barely even noticed the change from doing it on weekends to doing it most of the week. Dublin was flooded with heroin in the early 1980s, so by the middle of the decade there were these vigilante groups like Concerned Parents Against Drugs, and anyone suspected of being associated with heroin could get a bad beating. So there was that danger, but there was the added fact that I was getting well known through the band, so I came to an arrangement with this bloke who'd go and score the stuff for me. I'd give him money to get some for me and some for himself. He's since died of an overdose.

Over the course of a couple of years I was gradually using more and more, but I didn't see that as something I was making happen. As far as I was concerned it was just something that was happening. It had really nothing to do with me. I was running into heroin more and more in my daily life, but it didn't occur to me that the heroin wasn't running into me – that I was the one doing the running. I didn't realise it at the time, but I was forming an addiction.

Meanwhile, this drug that I saw as filling in the distance between me and the rest of the world was actually creating a distance between me and the people closest to me – my wife, my family and the rest of the band. The band liked to drink but I was never a drinker, so I didn't like that pub and club scene anyway. From the start, where we'd all given up our jobs for a common goal, we'd been a very close-knit bunch. We'd rehearsed together, toured together and hung out together. But without realising it, I became more secretive. I made excuses for why I couldn't be there for this or that. I knew there was a stigma to what I was doing, so I became furtive. And that's what heroin does – you gradually replace your real friends with unsavoury people. And the thing about it was I didn't even know I had a problem.

Things came to a head with the rest of the band when we arrived back in Ireland after doing a TV show in Germany and some gigs in England. In Germany I suddenly started feeling really shit and I couldn't function. The rest of the lads were concerned but suspicious. By the time we got to Birmingham to start a string of dates with Stiff Little Fingers, I thought I was coming down with something. The manager got me a doctor. The doctor gave me a check-up and said, 'There's nothing wrong with you.' I didn't believe him.

'There has to be *something* wrong with me,' I told him. 'I feel terrible.'

We landed in Dublin and there was a bus picking us up to head straight down the east coast to Waterford where we had a gig that night. I didn't think I could get through a gig, so I called a mate and said, 'Can you come down to Waterford, and can you bring a bit of that stuff? Maybe that'll make me feel better.' I still hadn't made the connection.

The mate couldn't make the gig. I just about got through it but my voice was in rag order and I was in bits. We stayed overnight in Waterford because the next day we had to do a signing appearance in the town. Aslan were really happening by now, we were flying, and there were all these kids looking for autographs. When we got to the signing I told the rest of the band I couldn't do it. I told them I had the worst pneumonia on earth and I didn't feel well enough. But then the mate from Dublin arrived and we ducked into a room and had a smoke.

I walked out of that room ten minutes later jumping cart-wheels: 'Now, what do you want on these autographs?'

And the rest of the band saw this sudden change and they went: 'Aw, fuck this!'

After the signing the others took me aside and told me they recognised the bloke who'd come down from Dublin and they knew what sort of scumbags I'd started to hang out with.

This stopped me in my tracks. I was honestly convinced that I'd been so clever that no one had a clue what I was doing. But even when this realisation was hitting me, I was telling myself that they were overreacting to a minor situation. They liked drink, I didn't. I preferred the buzz from a little smoke of heroin once in a while. Everything was on track. We'd got the record deal we'd been chasing for so long. We'd just come back from touring Britain with Stiff Little Fingers. We'd gone for the Bowie support slot at his upcoming Slane show, and we'd got that. We were on a roll. What were they whingeing about?

But we nearly split up that day in Waterford, and after a night's sleep the reality had sunk in that we'd come to a crunch. Everything we'd all worked so long for was in serious jeopardy. I sat down with the others and promised I was going to clean up my act. And I really meant it. I felt relief that they had confronted me, that I could now admit to myself that I had a problem, and that I'd stop. But it was only then, when I decided to stop, that I found out this was not the innocent recreational drug I'd told myself it was. I'd always told myself I'll stop when I want to stop, but now I found out that heroin didn't work like that. I still thought I could do it, though. I never even thought of confiding in Kathryn. I thought I could do it on my own.

22

The Tabloid Crucifixion
of Boy George

The Sun: 'GEORGE THE JUNKIE. EIGHT WEEKS TO LIVE!'
The Star: 'BOY GEORGE – AIDS RISK'

When I saw all that 'George the junkie' stuff in the English tabloids, I never, ever thought that it could happen over here. It never occurred to me, even though I'd been doing what Boy George was doing, which at that stage was smoking gear on the odd occasion. The English papers started going after Elton John at the same time, accusing him of being a gay pervert. I never thought that Boy George and Elton John were fair game just because they were big pop stars. I thought it was very unfair the way they were being treated by the tabloids, but I did think this was no more than you'd expect from the British press. It was a very British thing to build them up and then knock them down, but that had never happened here in Ireland. Then, when it did happen here for the very first time, it happened to *me*! I couldn't believe that I merited that kind of scrutiny. The one small comfort I took was the support I got from most of the Irish journalists, who were horrified by what was being done to me because they didn't want to see that sort of vicious journalism coming into Ireland.

'WILL GEORGE MICHAEL BE NEXT?'

Pop used to be safe from scrutiny by the English tabloids because it was a secret society, impenetrable to the disapproving adult gaze. But Eighties pop has no robes of mystery to hide within. Instead it has sacrificed itself on the altars of celebrity.

The London rumour mill is abuzz that the *News of the World* has its own exclusive on George Michael filed away for use – or abuse – at the most telling moment. The paranoia may be exaggerated but it typifies the fears that the carnage is not yet complete.

Bill Graham, 'Pop Go The Weasels', *Hot Press*, May 1987

23

Courting the Redtops: A Dangerous Game

Danny was born into the tabloid culture that existed in England for a long time before it arrived in Ireland. He grew up with that tabloid mentality, which was completely new to us. Something small would happen to the band and Danny would turn it into column inches. It's something Louis Walsh would become very good at. One time we opened the *Evening Herald* to learn to our horror that the master tapes for our first album had been stolen. We were freaked. We thought we were facing a real crisis, but it turned out a false alarm. What really happened was that there had been a break-in at the Aslan offices on the quays and all the thieves took was a ghetto blaster. We were in the middle of recording the album at the time and we'd given Danny a cassette tape with a few bits and pieces from the sessions for a listen. So when the break-in happened he put out this story that the master tapes were gone and that £100,000 of recording time had gone down the Swanee. He even told the press that because we'd spent a fortune recording them, we were willing to pay a ransom to get them back. Fake news was a Danny speciality.

Another time we were flying to a gig and the plane hit a bit of turbulence. This was years before we were in an actual plane crash, and it was nothing at all. But we opened the papers the next day to read that our flight had nearly come down in the middle of the Irish Sea. Our 'near thing' made the headlines years before the same thing happened with Boyzone. Danny was a real bullshitter, but he would get us great press.

We didn't see the danger of the game Danny was playing with the press – that *we* were playing with the press. We weren't seeing it from that perspective. We released an album that was well received and went straight to number one in Ireland. The singles were going to the top of the charts. The press were being kind to us. We didn't recognise Bill Graham's warnings about the viciousness and the treachery of tabloid culture as having anything to do with us. When it did happen I was shocked.

24

A Lad in Slane

The first outdoor concert at Slane Castle was 1981, when maybe 30,000 people turned up to see Thin Lizzy, with a little-known band called U2 at the bottom of the support bill. The following year the Rolling Stones played Slane and it really took off as Ireland's big summer event. Then there was Bob Dylan, followed by Bruce Springsteen, and then Queen in 1986.

I'd been at every Slane up to Bowie, starting with the first one in 1981 when Thin Lizzy headlined. Myself and some mates would all pile into a car and drive up there. After Lizzy finished their set we were trying to make a quick getaway, and by luck we just happened to get in behind an ambulance that was speeding back to Dublin, so we were able to follow the ambulance through the crowd and the traffic jams and we got back home in no time. The next year it was the Rolling Stones, and we copped that ambulances were leaving all the time to make a dash to hospital with people who'd collapsed or injured themselves, or drank themselves into a coma. I remember tailgating an ambulance away from the Stones concert as there were fireworks going off behind us in the sky above the castle. After the escape from the

Stones went so well we decided we'd do the same every year, waiting until an ambulance was leaving and then pulling in tight behind it to leave all the traffic jams behind.

We had just signed to EMI when we heard that David Bowie was to be the headliner at Slane for 1987. The moment we heard this we went to Danny and said that we didn't care if he never got us another gig, but he had to get us onto the bill for Bowie at Slane.

Four years earlier myself and some of Meelah XVIII had got the boat over to England to see Bowie's 'Serious Moonlight' tour at Milton Keynes. On the ferry there was this room like a small cinema with two big television screens. There were some oul wans in there watching some film on these tellies, but a load of us invaded the place and someone threw a champagne bottle through one of the screens. All the oul wans ran out and we got up and played a set of Bowie songs. We played for more than an hour. The people we'd thrown out must have reported us but no one took any action because there were too many of us, and nearly everyone on the boat were Bowie fans heading to Milton Keynes and they wanted to hear us playing. Shortly after we got back from the Bowie show, Meelah XVIII had a gig in the Ivy Rooms. On the posters we printed the message: 'Remember the Boat Trip', and the place was jammed!

So we said to Danny, 'We don't care about anything else. You can retire after this, but get us the Bowie gig.' Our worst nightmare, because we were true-blue Bowie fans, was that some other band would get the support, and as far as we were concerned, no one else deserved it.

He got us the gig, and I was never more terrified in my life than when we arrived in Slane early that day. We went backstage, just to get a feel of the place, and even that early in the day there was already a scattering of people out front. Then the time came for the gig and we opened with a song called 'The Gallery'. Alan would start it with a few *rat-a-tat-tats*, then Joe would come in, and then Tony, and as the song got going I'd make my entrance and start the vocals – I stole that bit of theatrics off Billy!

I ran out on stage with this picture still in my head from hours earlier of a few people out there, but this time the place was jammed. It was like walking out of a shop on a really breezy day and the wind just catches your breath. *Aha-haaa.* And I was terrified. I said to myself, this can go either one way or the other – I can freeze here or just get over it and get on with it.

The stage was at different levels and we were told that under no circumstances were we to go onto the level at the very front, because it had to be kept clean for Bowie's dancers. Up until now we'd been playing venues where you could see the whites of the punters' eyes. Now here we were in a big open-air hollow where the nearest audience member was twenty yards away, and I found it hard to connect. We were doing this song called 'Sands of Time' where a drum break goes into a guitar break – 1-2-3-4! – and at this point I could see Carlos Alomar and Peter Frampton watching us from the wings. They high-fived each other and I got a surge of adrenaline because they were signalling their approval, so I grabbed Billy and the two of us jumped down onto this forbidden section of the stage. From then on the gig really took off because we were right down within touching distance of the audience.

I'm no good at all the arse-licking that goes on after gigs, so when Bowie had finished his set I just wanted to get home on my own and think about what had just happened. I was driving back to Dublin thinking that this was a moment I'd been living for since the first time I saw David Bowie on *Top of the Pops*, and it's over, and I'm on my way home, and I didn't enjoy it. After that, to this day, every time I do something that I think is of any value, I pause and just soak it up and enjoy the moment.

It didn't help, driving back from Slane that night, that I'd never had a chance to meet Bowie. When he was going from the dressing room to the stage he was flanked by his band and crew, and every one of them was dressed in a uniform of grey boiler suits. There were maybe sixteen or twenty people walking in military formation, forming a block around Bowie who was walking at the centre of this formation. Because they were all dressed the same, you couldn't tell which one was Bowie unless you were very close. I was looking at this thinking that even as eccentric rock star behaviour goes, this was a bit weird.

A short while after I got home I had a call from the lads in the band saying they were in the Pink Elephant and that Bowie was there. So I followed them into the Pink and Bowie was cordoned off in the VIP section with his two huge ex-marine minders standing guard. Billy said he was going over to ask for his autograph. We begged him not to, it was so uncool, but he made off towards Bowie anyway until the two bouncers blocked his way with a wagging finger.

Billy was really pissed off that Bowie would treat him like that, after we'd played on the same stage a few hours earlier, but then, years later, we finally did get to meet Bowie. This time he'd just played Dublin's Point Depot, and Harry Crosbie, who owned the venue, threw an after-show party. I was surprised at how short Bowie was, because he always projected himself as tall. He was in great form that night. We told him how he'd turned away Billy in the Pink that night years earlier, and he said that he was very paranoid at that time. He was still thinking of the murder of his friend John Lennon, and as an Englishman in Ireland he felt particularly vulnerable. The Troubles were still raging when he played Slane, and he said his paranoia explained the heavy security at the gig and the military convoy from the dressing room to the stage. He was apologetic about the whole thing.

25

Living it Large on 80
Pounds a Week

Even after signing to EMI we were still only bringing home a meagre wage of 80 pounds a week, but for most things we didn't have to put our hands in our pockets because Danny saw to it that everything was taken care of – out of our future earnings, of course.

We went to this fancy hairdresser's in Dublin city centre where we had a tab. We also had a taxi account that we could ring any time to go anywhere. And we had a tab at Dublin's hippest nightclub, the Pink Elephant. But at that time we were rehearsing all day every day for our debut album, so we didn't do a lot of socialising. Sometimes, at the end of a long day in the studio, people might feel like going to the Pink for a few pints because it was eleven o'clock at night and the pubs were shut. Billy and Tony and Alan were into that star-tripping thing. They loved going to the Pink but I was never into that scene. I hated the drinking culture, and the Pink Elephant was a step beyond even that. The music writer George Byrne was always there, and he was great because he'd create havoc. He'd spot some celeb and he'd lash them out of it! I didn't know George well at the time but I'd set myself up near his table so I could see what would happen, and with George something would *always* happen.

During this star-tripping phase, Joe was the one always telling everyone else to keep it together, but at the same time he was developing an obsession with Kinder Surprises. We had a bus that we'd use all the time for playing down the country, and there were 1,000 little Kinder Surprise toys on the dashboard put there by Joe. Joe was always a little separate from the rest of us, in his head anyway. So he'd be up the front making his little toys and we'd be sitting in the back taking the piss out of him. His behaviour around this time got him the nickname Doctor Strangepork from the rest of us.

The Forget Me Nots were touring Ireland at the same time as us. At the end of a gig in the most remote part of Donegal they'd all cram into their Hiace van and drive back to Dublin in the small hours. We wouldn't. We'd stay in a hotel. I remember myself and Billy talking to a couple of them and asking what they were up to with this driving through the night thing.

They said that when they'd come to be re-signed the next year, the record company was going to be very pleased to have spent only, say, 30 grand as opposed to 80 grand. I said to them, 'If you're a hit band, it won't matter what you've spent, and if you're not, you'll be dropped anyway. So just live the life while you can.'

And that's what we did, because we knew that if we had

a hit album, a few hotel nights would be a pittance in the bigger scheme of things, and by this time in the late 1980s bands were dropping like flies from their labels. In Tua Nua had been dropped. Blue in Heaven had been dropped. Cactus World News. Les Enfants. I knew the bass player with one of the dropped bands, and he was living with this beautiful model girlfriend. The band were away on tour when the news they'd been dropped broke in Ireland. The bass player arrived home to find his suitcases stacked outside the door of the apartment block. The model girlfriend had already moved onwards and upwards. A short time later she'd social-climbed her way to the top of the pop pile.

26

A Word to the Wise from Slade's Noddy Holder

ELECTRIC BALLROOM, CAMDEN TOWN

Aslan's previous London visits saw them do the rounds of the small pub and club circuit. Tonight saw them in their element, facing a packed audience in the roomy interior of the Electric Ballroom. This was a turning point. They went for the throat from the start, kicking off with 'Can't Hold Back'. A fiery version of new single 'Please Don't Stop' ably demonstrated to the London audience what we've known here all along – dammit, these boys are superstars!

Enda Murray, *Hot Press*, November 1987

There was this bloke called Pete the Terrible who used to put on an Irish week every year at the Mean Fiddler in London. There'd be ourselves, Mary Coughlan, Blue in Heaven, all these acts playing the festival, and we'd all be staying at the Columbia Hotel. One day Noddy Holder and Dave Hill from Slade were sitting at the bar having a pint. They were heroes to us. Myself and Tony had been having a joint at the bar, and we went up to Noddy and

Dave. We were trying to be cool and we said, 'Do you want a toke, man?'

And Noddy Holder says: 'Left it behind me years ago, son, and I'd advise you to do the same.'

We got talking to the pair of them and Noddy goes into a spiel about how you go into a rehearsal stoned one day and come out thinking you've written *Dark Side of the Moon*, and then you come back in the next day straight and sober and you listen back and it's the greatest pile of crap. And, to be honest, that used to happen to us a lot.

After those words of advice from the great Noddy Holder, Tony made a complete stop to grass and hash. Tony never did anything after that. As for me, I didn't take his advice on board for one second. My reaction was: 'What are you on about?' In fact, the more important the occasion, the more I came to rely on artificial sources of inspiration or Dutch courage. We might have a big gig, or a TV slot, or a meeting with someone from the record company who was going to have a big say on our career. Say, for instance, we had to go for a meal with some music biz executives. I'd tell myself that if I have a bit of gear I'll be in top form, but if I don't have it I'll be of no use to anyone. So I'd tell the others in the band that I had something I needed to do and I'd be half-an-hour late. The trouble is that even while you're telling yourself that this will only take half-an-hour, you know it probably won't. Then you get there to score and the bloke doesn't show up, and you *know* you're not going anywhere until he arrives. So you turn up for the important business meal and you're in great form but the meal is nearly finished and everybody's tired and the other band members are really pissed off.

It wasn't just important meetings I was missing. It was a day-to-day thing. I was arriving late for rehearsals and the excuses were wearing thin with the others. I'd rub my hand on the underneath of the car and park it somewhere out of sight. Then I'd arrive and tell them I'd had a puncture on the way over to the studio, and I'd show the muck on my hand as proof. Then, when the rehearsal was over, one of the lads would ask if I needed a lift and I'd ask why, having forgotten the story about the puncture that I'd told them a few hours earlier.

It pissed them off even more on days when I couldn't get any gear and I had to turn up for rehearsals strung out. I'd arrive late because I'd spent the morning trying to score, and then I'd be useless when I got there because I was sick, and then I'd make some bullshit excuse to leave early. It got to the point where I had just two things to do every day. One was to get straight, the other was to make it to rehearsal, but if it came down to one over the other there was no contest. The gear came first, and my justification to myself was that if I went in sick I was going to be of no use to anybody anyway. But I *was* going in sick, even on days I did score. I'd have a smoke in the car and stroll in to start rehearsals and I'm on top of the world for the first while, but before we're even halfway through I'm fading fast, my eyelids are drooping, my voice is gone. But all the time in my little cocoon I feel that I'm in charge of the situation, I've got them all fooled. But I didn't have them all fooled, and it was all building.

For a while, hiding my addiction from Kathryn was easier than hiding it from the band. Kathryn was still working full-time as a hairdresser, so by the time she arrived home most evenings I'd have done all my running about and I'd be sorted for the rest of the day. The lads in the band knew what I was up to but they tried to avoid confrontation. With Kathryn, she didn't confront me because, bad as I was getting, she really didn't know. And bad as I was getting, things would get a lot worse.

For the moment, though, everyone focused on the immediate business in hand – recording our debut album, *Feel No Shame*. After sounding out a few producers we met Mick Glossop in Waterford and went for a meal with him, and we thought he was fairly cool. We picked him because we hit it off straight away, but also because of his track record as the producer of The Waterboys' *This Is the Sea*, plus Van Morrison, Magazine and other artists we liked. In the studio he was very school-teachery, but we were willing to learn. He was also very frugal. We were recording the album in Dublin city centre and he was staying in the Gresham on Stephen's Green. There was a pub on Pearse Street about half a mile from the Gresham that sold a pint for a penny less than the surrounding pubs, and he used to walk to that pub in rundown Pearse Street. Mick bought this state-of-the-art drum machine and then rented it out to us for the duration of recording the album, so we must have paid for it ten times over!

27

Feel No Shame Hits
Number One in Ireland

The first thing you're asked about in an interview is U2. What connection have you got to U2? What do you know about U2? What skeletons have they got in the cupboard? And you get really sick of it. I realise the help that the focus U2 have put on Ireland has been. In one way it's a stepping stone to get you off the ground, but in another it's a disadvantage because of the bullshit you have to go through after that.

'Christy: "I've Nothing Against U2"', *Hot Press* cover story,
March 1988

When the single 'Feel No Shame' went straight to number one we got the cover of *Hot Press*, Ireland's counterpart to the *New Musical Express* or *Rolling Stone*. It was just me on the cover. That was the deal. The band handed that over to me. We delegated different jobs to different people and my job was doing interviews and some photoshoots. If a band has a message to put across, it's much easier to put it across via one individual, because people can relate much easier to one person than to a group. At first I was worried that the others wouldn't be getting as much recognition, even though they were putting in the same amount of work as me, but that was something we all came to accept very early on.

I don't know if it did cause some build-up of resentment. It's not something that ever came to light. Doing the *Feel No Shame* photoshoot I brought in Kiera, who was just a little baby, while Joe brought in his baby daughter who was about the same age. We took photos with me holding both babies, but Joe's daughter wouldn't settle, as she didn't know me. So it ended up being Kiera as the final cover image, which made sense given the father and son themes of *Feel No Shame*.

We'd released the album, which went straight to the top of the Irish charts, and we had a German tour booked. Myself and Billy went to Germany for a round of pre-tour publicity slots. We arrived in Munich and there were two limousines waiting for us. They put Billy into one and me into the other. We got to the Munich Hilton Hotel and into our separate rooms, and I've got a four-poster bed. So I flop down on the bed and start messing with the little control beside the bed and I hear this buzzing, but I can't figure out where it's coming from. Then I look up and the roof of the bed is coming down, and the curtains pull across at the side, and lights come on, and it's after turning into a sunbed!

I said to Billy that they must think we're the Pet Shop Boys, who were huge everywhere at the time. We didn't respect the fact that we'd had a number one in Ireland because, we told ourselves, it's *only* Ireland. But as far as the Germans were concerned, we were number one in a country, and they didn't care if that country was Ireland or America or Japan or the Isle of Man. As far as they were concerned we were a number one band.

When you're a young fella from a place like Finglas, and you've been on the labour, and nobody's ever expected anything of you except that you were reared to become a mechanic or electrician at best, and now everybody wants to be seen with you – it does turn your head a little, especially if you're young and immature. That's what happened to us. That's where the star-tripping thing came in. It's true what they say, that you should never believe your own publicity. The reason they give that warning is that people fall into this trap all the time. I don't think I was as bad as some members of the band, but it does turn you because you're in a false environment.

The business machine actually surrounds you with people whose job it is to make you believe your own publicity. We were in the London EMI offices just after the album came out, and they were showing us the press cuttings of the reviews. Here's the *Melody Maker* review and it's great. And here's what the *NME* said, and it's great too. Then I asked for the clipping from *Sounds* or *Smash Hits* or some other mag I was interested in, and I was told, 'Ah no, it's not in yet.' What we found out later was that the press office would only show us the good reviews, because they'd get their arses kicked by their department boss over any bad reviews. Their job was to know who, in every publication, was the right person to get a record to for review. It was their job to get it into the hands of someone who was going to like it, instead of, let's say, the heavy metal specialist.

Based on the reviews we were fed by the press office, we thought that everybody in the world loved our album universally. So you're put in this false environment where everybody is showing you respect. A couple of years earlier we were dropping tapes in to the top radio DJs like Dave Fanning and Gerry Ryan, begging for just a single play or even a mention on air. Now their people are phoning you up saying, 'Can you come in for an interview?'

I've always undermined whatever achievements we've had. I think it's an insecurity that I personally have. And looking back, what we did was huge. We were the first Irish band to have our debut album go straight in at number one. We were the first Irish band to have two singles simultaneously in the Top 10. These are records that can't ever be broken because we were the first to do it. So if anyone does it tomorrow it doesn't matter – we were there first. There were all these achievements that we didn't recognise at the time. Then we went to Germany thinking we meant nothing there, and we're going to have to start at the bottom, playing their equivalent of the Ivy Rooms. But then we got there and we were given the star treatment. We were shocked, but when it happened we enjoyed it to the full.

28

Star-Trippin' Across the USA

In the summer of 1988 we finally arrived in the USA for our first tour going coast to coast. The purpose of the trip was twofold. Half of it was to get ourselves seen by American audiences, while the other half was to meet and greet the record company executives, record pluggers and radio jocks who'd be giving us the big push. For a lot of the shows we were playing with Graham Parker, who'd recently parted ways with his famous backing band The Rumour. It was 60 grand to buy onto the Graham Parker tour and we had to bring an extra 20 grand in cash for tips. That money was advanced by the record company. The way it works is that you look at the artists touring America who might be a good fit for your type of music and for the type of audience you're trying to reach. Obviously we weren't looking to tour with a thrash metal outfit like Megadeth, because that wouldn't be our audience. There were big acts touring who would have suited us, but because it was our first time in the States we were too small for those. By too small I mean that the record company wasn't yet prepared to pay over the serious amounts of money required to buy us onto one of those big-name tours.

Graham Parker seemed like a good fit for Aslan. He wasn't metal, he wasn't punk, his band were into good rock music and we thought his audience would appreciate us. So we told our record company we'd like Graham Parker, and they were given a figure of $60,000 to get us on the tour. Part of that was to cover the cost of our gear being transported along with their gear. The venues were good prestige places, like the Fillmore West in San Francisco. The arrangement was that we'd do the big shows with Parker and we'd play our own smaller headlining gigs along the way.

We flew out of London for the States. We were in all our leather gear up front in business class getting dirty looks from all these snooty types in their bespoke suits. But then we came out the other end in New York and the men in suits were all getting into these smelly yellow cabs and we're stepping into limousines, and it was fuck you!

One of the first things I wanted to do in New York was taste an American burger, an American pizza and a genuine hot dog. As soon as we arrived at our hotel we sent one of the crew out to get five large pizzas. He came back with these five huge breadboards. So we discovered on day one that when you want pizza in the States you buy a slice of pizza. One pizza fed the whole band, leaving us with four we couldn't eat, so we went knocking on people's doors up and down the corridor asking did they want half a pizza. Most of them were startled. This was not what they'd expected checking into one of New York's most exclusive hotels.

We travelled across America in a tour bus, and at the front you had a little kitchen, then a few seats, then bunk beds on either side, and then at the very back there was a lounge with a TV, a video player and all that. Nowadays, with digital technology, it's easy to have a TV in your car, but back then this was state-of-the-art high-end luxury. If you wanted to see America the way we got to see America it would cost a fortune. I remember driving through the Mojave Desert and it was like gliding through a cowboy film. Mind-blowing.

The messing with the cocaine and champagne started straight away in New York. One of the record company execs bought us a couple of grammes of coke and two bottles of champagne. Next stop was Boston, where they asked us did so-and-so look after us in New York, and we said yeah, he bought us two grammes of coke and two bottles of champagne. So the guy in Boston bought us four grammes of coke and four bottles of champagne. So this little light went on in our heads. *Ding!* And by the time we got to Los Angeles a few weeks later we were destroyed.

And that's sort of what led to the split. I've briefly mentioned before that when we came back from America all the rest of the band stopped. For them, the trip had been a great little holiday but it was time to get back to work. But because I had the addictive thing in me I couldn't stop, I had to keep going.

I came back from that first American trip with my eyes opened. I knew how hard it was going to be to crack the States. When we were over there, 'Loving Me Lately' was released as our first US single. We got a video play on MTV on a thing called 'Hit Or Miss', and it came in as a miss, and I thought, this isn't going to be easy. With Graham Parker we went from a big place like the Fillmore in San Francisco to the next gig in Cleveland, which was the size of the Baggot Inn. Parker had sold a lot of albums in the States. He'd had Top 40 hits. Bruce Springsteen had sung backing vocals for him. And that's where I realised you can be massive in one state and mean nothing in the next state along. Then there's the sheer size of America. It makes Europe seem small.

Billy wasn't into the drug benders. We were staying in a hotel in Boston and a top English band I won't name were staying in the same place. We got up the morning after the first of our two gigs there and the other band were heading back to England. Billy climbs onto our tour bus with a little package of white powder and says the English lads didn't want to bring it back through customs so we could have it. So myself and our road manager grabbed it and snorted it, thinking it was cocaine. It was Andrews Liver Salts! There was white froth bubbling out from our noses and mouths.

*

We arrived back in Ireland and all our focus was on a big open-air show in the heart of Dublin to mark the city's millennium. It was a time when every one-horse town in the country was inventing an anniversary for itself so they could throw a party and hopefully attract tourist revenue. In the space of a couple of years you had Cork's 800th birthday, Galway's 500th, and now someone had decided that Dublin was to have a year of parties to celebrate reaching 1,000 years old in 1988. They just pulled a figure out of the air!

In the back garden, just after we moved to Finglas. Ma, Da, myself (with the bald head) and my older sister Bernie (with the panda).

Bernie's first communion day. Ma, Da, James in Ma's arms, Bernie in her communion dress, Deirdre and me.

Da would sing old opera songs while carving the Sunday roast. Therese and Jackie are telling him to hurry up and get it on the table.

Ma and Da in the living room. Ma cuddles Da, while Da cradles Eddie – the youngest and 18 years my junior.

Me on the same sofa, sometime in the late '70s.

Me and Kathryn hanging out in the late '70s or very early '80s.

Kathryn with baby Kiera, aged one, in 1988.

Aslan around 1985 posing in a field in Finglas. Finglas was famous for its stray horses and a couple strayed into the background.

Me looking moody on Sandymount beach in south Dublin, with the city's iconic twin stacks in the distance.

For years I performed barefoot. What started out as a trick to avoid tripping on leads quickly turned into a superstitious good luck ritual.

The band reunited in the early '90s to play the annual summer Finglas Festival.

A happy looking Aslan line-up featuring (l-r) Billy, Tony, me, Alan and Joe. © Hot Press

An early shot of myself and Billy giving it loads at a festival. Attempts by the record label to market the pair of us like the Black & White whiskey ad of the time were ill-judged and caused ill-feeling.

Looking dead cool in a pool hall for our first big *Hot Press* spread. © Hot Press

Me with face fungus clutching a copy of our Number
One debut album, *Feel No Shame*. © Hot Press

Aslan, with a changed line-up, performing at London's Shepherds Bush Empire in 2012, shortly before I was laid low by illness. © Getty

Playing Dublin's Vicar Street in 2018. Playing live again anywhere seemed wishful thinking during two years in hospital and in a wheelchair. © JB Photography

The wedding party. Myself and Kathryn, together with the best legacy we could leave: Kiera and Darren, with their kids Cian and Ava (no Jake yet).

Deep breath now for a big family shot of Arron, Eric, Matthew, Luke, Ellen, Kiera, Ava, Da, Kitty (my goddaughter in Ma's arms), Shane, Karl, Christopher (my nephew) and Cian. This is the last photo of my ma with the whole family.

Father and daughter singing from the same hymn sheet on *The Late Late Show* in 2018. It wasn't a hymn, though, it was 'Under Pressure'.

Four generations of Dignams: Jackie, Kathryn, Da, Shane, Bernie, me, Kiera, Cian and Ava. This was the first Christmas at Da's after Ma passed away.

Christy Dignam The Next Generation (two actually): Cian, Darren, Kiera, Jake and Ava enjoying the sun in the summer of 2019.

The highlight of the birthday celebrations was a huge out-door gig in a car park in the city centre, and Aslan were the headliners. We sent limousines to Finglas to pick up my ma and granny and the rest of the family. I can still picture my ma in that limo and she was just beaming with pride. We got loads of grief in the press and from other bands for indulging in rock'n'roll excess, but I'd do it all exactly the same if I had the chance again. It was one of the most positive things about being in a band – just being able to do that.

This was a vital gig for us. A load of executives had come over from the States to watch. It was in the very centre of Ireland's capital city and this was the perfect setting for us to deliver the message to the Americans: 'Okay, you've seen us over there, but now see how big we are over here.' This was a crucial show for us, not just for the day that it was on, but for our whole future.

We knew that a great deal would rest on the impact we made on the visiting executives, but we thought we could let our music do the talking and, in truth, we were not in any awe of these people coming over from Los Angeles because we'd already seen them up close. Whereas other bands would have played the game and brought them for fine dining in the Trocadero, we brought them to a pub on Sheriff Street, which was at the derelict heart of Dublin's urban decay in the 1980s. We liked pulling the piss out of people, but we weren't doing it out of laddishness. We were doing it out of our sense of absurdity of the way the whole thing works. Take the music magazines, for instance. They give you a poxy review one week, then you take out an expensive two-page advert and the next review is glowing. The whole thing was absurd.

As it turned out the Americans loved the trip to Sheriff Street, because if you're an American of a certain class you never see that kind of existence. You might pass close by it in the projects of New York, but high-flying executives from LA would never be exposed to anything like that. We'd built a really good relationship with them when we were in the States, because half of them had Irish roots and they were delighted to have an Irish act on their books.

Danny pushed in us that sense of not being part of the common herd. When we started off we didn't realise that we were different, that we had a different kind of energy, a different vibe to all those identikit Irish bands coming off the 'next U2' production line. When I had my first run-in with Danny he was kind of impressed with our attitude and he magnified that side of us.

The irony of ironies is that of all the people we did give too much respect to it was Danny. We gave him more respect than he deserved because we thought he knew what he was doing. We thought, what do we know? We're only five eejits from Finglas.

Danny was on 20 per cent of all our earnings. Not only was he on 20 per cent of the revenue from our gigs, he was also on 20 per cent of our contracts. So if we were signing a record deal for 60 grand, he was getting 20 per cent of that while we were on a weekly wage.

We didn't sign a management contract with Danny Kenny in the first place because it just never came up. I've heard stories that we didn't formalise it because his existing band,

Cactus World News, were jealous he'd taken us on too. I don't think they were jealous, and even if they were, that had nothing to do with us not signing a contract. Things just happened so quickly that we were all happy to go along at first on a trust basis. Then, as time went on, I think maybe we didn't sign a contract because he was a bit of a party animal and we were a bit wary of all that. In the end I think we didn't want to sign to him for ten years and then discover we were after tying an anchor to ourselves.

On top of that I had serious doubts about whether Danny was right to represent us in America. In England all the record company heads were blokes like us. They were young fellas and they looked like us, they dressed like us, they were cool like us. But we got to America and we were dealing with suits. They were businessmen. The music came a long way second to the business of making money. It was totally different.

Just a few weeks before our big homecoming show for Dublin's 1000th birthday, we did two gigs in the legendary Roxy on LA's Sunset Strip. Danny was in full party mode and I could see these record company businessmen in their Armani suits wearing disapproving looks. And we were thinking, these guys are investing a lot of money in us and to my eyes it was plain as day they were not impressed.

I talked to the band about that when it happened. I told them that the suits in America didn't like his attitude. When we got back from the States I was saying to the band that Danny's 'let's party' attitude wasn't helping to create a good impression of the band, and he would have got wind of that.

I'm not saying that this was a factor in me being forced out of the band – I've no evidence for that – but I'm allowed to have my views.

It wasn't like I wanted to party on when we arrived back in Ireland. I was addicted. I didn't see drugging as partying. From a cocaine perspective you could see it as a party thing, but heroin is different; I was just maintaining. For me to just get up in the morning I had to use gear. Looking back at it, there were also all these compromises we had to make and all these people getting between us – the five people who made up the band. When I used heroin I could tolerate a lot of that stuff. Take for instance the Black & White whisky thing that EMI were trying to push with me and Billy.

The whisky company was running a huge marketing campaign at the time featuring two dogs – a black Scottish terrier and a West Highland white. As far as I could see, EMI were trying to market me and Billy as a rock version of Wham! in a parody of the whisky ad campaign – me with the black hair and him with the dyed white hair, and all the chains hanging from his leather jacket. They were promoting me and Billy as equals but, to me, I was the lead singer of the band and Billy was the backing vocalist who contributed a few harmonica lines. So I asked the EMI people what were they trying to do, and they told me: 'Look, it's a great image, just go with it.' I didn't want to just go with it.

Billy will admit himself that at that point he was probably the least musically inclined of the five of us, so for him to be put at the forefront of the band was a big thing for him. He's since come on to where he is now as a musician, and his character is intrinsic to the band. Back then it wasn't, but the marketing men were pushing him to the front. And at the same time as they were pushing Billy into the foreground they were shoving Joe into the background, and he was musically the main man in the band. Myself, Tony and Joe were doing all the writing, but when it came to the press end of things, myself and Billy were pushed to the forefront.

But that's record companies. While we were in the States I was in the audience for Graham Parker with one of the record company guys. Parker was playing 'Hey Lord, Don't Ask Me Questions', and I told the guy beside me that I loved that song. The record company guy says back, 'He's a dinosaur, man, a fucking dinosaur. You kids are what's happening.' And I'm listening to this thinking, the fucking cheek of you. Graham Parker has made you millions, and now he's no longer making you millions, as far as you're concerned he's just a wanker. While I do think that the sexual abuse in my childhood had a lot to do with my addiction, I think having to live in the music business environment accelerated it. I was doing press interviews eight hours a day, where one interviewer is wheeled in for twenty minutes followed by another, then another. You lose track, and you're asking the interviewer if you've already told them this or that ten minutes ago. You end up trying to manufacture enthusiasm, and that's really hard, but when you took gear that made it easier to be false and just go along with things.

29

The Door's Kicked In, The Sky Falls In

There was this guy called Paschal Boland who had a flat on Clonliffe Avenue near Croke Park. I knocked down to him one Saturday morning, and when I rang the doorbell he threw the keys down to me so I could open the front door and come up the stairs. I arrived into his flat and I was standing with my back to the door as he handed me a batch of ten quarters of gear so I could pick the two biggest ones. I was in the process of picking when I heard a key in the door behind me. I said to him, 'Is that your door?' but he said, 'Ah no, that's downstairs.'

With that, the door came in on top of me. Next thing I'm flat on the floor with a gun to my head and handcuffs on my wrists and there's cops everywhere. It was Nóirín O'Sullivan who led the raid. Years later she'd rise to become the Garda Commissioner, Ireland's top cop. To be fair to her, after busting me she tried to help me by putting me in touch with a doctor who put me on a methadone course. The band were happening and I think her attitude was that I had everything ahead of me and I didn't need all this low-life shit I was getting myself into. She genuinely wanted to help.

There was another guy in the room called Christopher, who's dead now. The three of us were brought to Fitzgibbon Street Garda Station and they said to Paschal, 'This is the deal, Paschal. This is your gaff, that's your gear, and you're getting done, end of story. You can put your hands up for it and we can let the other two go, or we can charge the three of you. One way or another you're getting charged for this.' And credit where it's due, he put his hands up and said it was his gear. So that was that, or so I thought, but it wasn't the end of the matter. It was just the beginning.

A short while later we were rehearsing songs for the second album at Ropewalk Studios in Ringsend, and I picked up Alan one morning to drive him to the studio. We got to Ropewalk and there was nobody there, so I asked Alan if I'd got my times right because I was usually late and it was unusual for me to be first there. Alan said, 'Yeah, we're right on time.'

So I rang the office and Danny answered and I told him there was no one at the studio and he said, 'Yeah, well, you're out of the band.' He said that Tony, Joe and Billy were there with him and they wanted me out. So I said, 'Right, I'll be over there in five minutes.'

So I jumped in the car and headed to the band's office on Bachelors Walk, but while I was heading there, Billy, Joe and Tony were travelling in the opposite direction to Ropewalk. They hadn't the balls to face me.

I arrived and there was just Danny waiting for me.

'That's it, you're sacked. You're strung out and the band want you out, blah blah blah.'

Word of the Clonliffe bust had reached the others through the Ballymun grapevine. I was devastated. From the age of sixteen I was always the one who'd been the instigator. I was the one who put together Meelah XVIII and then broke up that band to form Aslan. I was the one who assembled all the musicians. I was the one who'd go out to RTÉ and sit outside the gate for hours handing tapes to people. I was the one knocking on the doors of *Hot Press* and *In Dublin* with demo tapes for them to review. I was the one who arranged all the showcase gigs for the record companies. Now all that work was gone.

For years while we struggled to get signed Kathryn had supported me, and when we signed I was able to come home and tell her, 'Kathryn, you can finally take your foot off the pedal – I'm taking over now.' And now, here I was facing the horrible prospect of going back to Kathryn and telling her she was in charge of the finances again. All I could think of was how am I going to tell Kathryn?

But before I could tell Kathryn anything, Danny rang her and said, 'Christy's out of the band.'

She was shocked. She asked him what was going on.

'Christy's strung out,' he told her straight.

She'd never heard the term 'strung out'. She didn't know what it meant.

Kathryn got cervical cancer when Kiera was a young baby. She had to undergo treatment that left her totally drained, and she was convalescing from that when she got the double whammy from Danny, telling her I was out of the band *and* I had a heroin habit. She wasn't wholly herself to be able to deal with any sort of a bang. She was in a weakened state. I remember driving up Pearse Street on the way home to face her that day, knowing she was not well. I felt so small. I had to walk in the front door and tell her I'd fucked up everything. I had to tell her not only have I fucked up and lost everything that we've worked for, Kathryn, and not only have I brought this down on you when you're not well enough to handle it, but I'm also a heroin addict, and we have to deal with that too. It was the lowest point of my life. Everything that I'd promised her, I'd broken.

There were all these things to say. I didn't even know where to start.

She just embraced me.

That's Kathryn. That's who she is, and I don't know how she does it. Her attitude was, 'Right, we're in this situation, where do we go from here?'

Kathryn got a second phone call days later telling her to come into the office to collect my passport and stuff. She'd had some time to gather herself and steel herself, and she got there ready to give them a piece of her mind, but they wouldn't even let her up to the office. Danny's office was above an antiques shop, and they left my stuff in the shop below because they didn't want to face her. The whole thing was deeply disrespectful to her. The whole split was very acrimonious and very bitter.

I went back to Danny to ask what was really going on, thinking there might be a way to save the situation. He said he didn't know, and maybe right then he didn't know.

And when it came down to the final say, the decision *was*

made by the other lads. EMI had said, 'We'll put him in rehab. We'll get him the best treatment money can buy. You can travel in different cars from Christy. We'll put him in different hotels when you're touring. It's not a big deal, it happens all the time in this business. It's only a small blip; we can sort it out. If you don't keep Christy, you don't keep the deal.'

At the time I had high hopes that the band would go for that separate lives solution, but in hindsight I can see it would never have worked because at that point I was only starting in my addiction. Anybody who's ever dealt with addiction will tell you that you really have to hit rock bottom before you can truly start on recovery. Otherwise you come back from the brink and you're thinking, okay, this time I fucked up a little bit, but now I know how to do it. Next time I won't make that mistake. You fool yourself, telling yourself all these things.

Had we gone with that arrangement of the separate hotels and the separate lives I would definitely be dead by now. I'd have killed myself with drugs because I would have kept the rock'n'roll lifestyle. The way things played out, when I did hit rock bottom my finances were fairly depleted, and that put a limit on the harm I could do myself. If I'd been in a position where I'd had no money problems I'd have killed myself without a shadow of a doubt.

I felt totally betrayed at the time but, looking back, the band had no option but to throw me out. When Aslan started, and in the long build-up to getting the record deal with EMI, I was the driving force within the band. I was the one with the ideas and the energy. And in a fairly short space of time it had gone from me being the main motivator to me contributing nothing. I was contributing nothing to the songwriting. My voice was gone. I was half the singer I'd been just a short time before. It was like a marriage. The band were the other half of that marriage and they were going through hell. They were suffering because of what I'd stopped putting into the marriage, but even more so because they had the same dreams that I had and I was fucking over their dreams. I was putting their dreams in jeopardy – the ones they'd worked so hard for. I was 100 per cent in the wrong, and they did precisely the right thing for themselves. More than likely they did what was best for me too, because I'm alive today.

Rejecting this separate lives offer from the record company, the others begged for a three-month reprieve. They told EMI they had a plan – they had a replacement singer lined up to jump in. He was going to be better than me. He was better-looking than me.

If you ask me what I think was going on in their heads – and this is just my opinion and not something I know for a fact – it's that at this time The Pogues were going into America after the success of 'Fairytale of New York' and they were trying to do it with the former Clash frontman Joe Strummer in place of Shane MacGowan, who wasn't functioning. They tried, but in the end they failed. The Pogues were already established with Shane as the frontman on 'Fairytale' because the video was so well known. It didn't work for The Pogues but the idea was still valid, and Aslan didn't have an instantly recognisable calling card like 'Fairytale'.

Aslan's replacement for me was Eamo Doyle. Eamo was real good-looking. He was a male model. They reckoned they could tour *Feel No Shame* in the States with Eamo as their singer and no one would know the difference. And for a very short while it seemed like it might work. They did an English tour and they were doing interviews, and they weren't giving any hints that Eamo wasn't the singer on the album. But the record company saw where it was going. The record executives gave them a chance to prove the new line-up with two showcase gigs, and then dropped them.

I've already said I felt deeply betrayed by what happened and I carried that anger for a long time. I couldn't believe it! I couldn't believe that mates would do this to another mate. There were loads of bands going around at the time where all the members seemed to be interchangeable pieces in an engine. If they weren't happy with their bass player they'd put an ad in *Hot Press* for a replacement bass player. We weren't like that, and I couldn't get my head around it. I felt 100 per cent betrayed. I was just devastated.

I was left totally on my own. They had the office, the record deal, the manager, everything. I walked away with nothing. Even when we signed the deal, they all got new amps and guitars and drums and whatever. I didn't get a golden microphone. I got nothing.

I remember walking away thinking I have nothing to show for the last five years. Yes, I have an album, but now even that is *their* album. Everything is theirs. It was horrendous. Then it got much, much worse.

30

You're Fired!

The Tabloid Crucifixion of Christy Dignam: Day One

The first of the three big *Star* attacks on me came with the
front-page headline 'ASLAN: IT'S THE END'. That pissed off
Danny Kenny. He didn't want to see this front-page headline
screaming that the band was over. He wanted my departure to be seen as a little hiccough in the career of Aslan.
He wanted it to be seen as nothing more than changing a
drum skin.

I'd been sacked a couple of weeks before *The Star*

145

were told that I'd been thrown out of the band, but during that time Danny had been telling me he was on my side. His instructions were: 'Don't say anything to anyone about the split. If the press contact you, deny everything.' He told me to let him talk to the band and we'd get through this. That the band were just pissed off at the moment.

What he was saying, as far as I understood him, was to say nothing, leave it to him, and he would hopefully turn the thing back.

So when the press approached me I would ask them what they were talking about. I'd say there was no split and no story because that's what I was told to say.

So when the story I thought he himself had fed to *The Star* came out under the headline 'ASLAN: IT'S THE END', that freaked Danny out. As I've already said, Danny wanted my departure to be seen as just a little hiccough on Aslan's trajectory to superstardom. He didn't reckon on *The Star* taking the stance that the band was gone, which would have meant his ride to the big time was gone.

When I read the paper that first morning, which was just about the split, I still felt that the whole situation could be salvaged. After all, you didn't expect anything more from *The Star*. But all this stuff about how they'd broken the news to me was bullshit because I was told in the office well before *The Star* got the story. I'd denied it up to that point because I thought Danny was on my side and he'd told me to deny everything.

When that first story appeared I thought it was the last of

it. I thought the next mention would be a couple of days later, saying Aslan are back together again. Then, the next day, all hell broke loose.

The Tabloid Crucifixion of Christy Dignam: Day Two

'I TOOK HEROIN,' SACKED ASLAN LEAD SINGER OPENS HIS HEART TO *THE STAR*

Sacked Aslan singer Christy Dignam last night admitted he has taken heroin. But he said he has not touched it for at least six months. He also denied his past experiments with drugs had anything to do with him being kicked out of the band . . . He says the real reason he was dumped was because he wanted more social comment in his songs.

Irish Star, 8 September 1988

I can't say for a fact who it was that told *The Star* I'd taken heroin, but several people close to those events have told me who it was and I've no reason to doubt them. That put *The Star* onto the whole drugs thing and they sent their people out to Ballymun and other places looking for dirt. People I had never met in my entire life were telling them, 'Yeah, I sold heroin to Christy.' *The Star* contacted me and said they had a story about me and heroin and they were going to run it the next day, so I might as well give my version.

Friends in the music biz put me in touch with a solicitor and the solicitor said that damage limitation was the best way to go. Just admit I had a slip, that I did use heroin, but that it was the worst thing I'd ever done. I should tell them I was really sorry and it was all in the past. So I did sit down with *The Star* and I admitted to having a bit of a thing with heroin in the past, but I insisted it wasn't the cause of the split. I was still focused on the band split because that was the important thing in my life. It was only as things unfolded that I realised the band split was a tiny side issue to the story they really wanted to write.

I was living in Finglas at the time and after the paper came out on day two, saying I'd taken heroin, there were cameramen with zoom lenses outside the gaff. First they went up to the door of Kathryn's mother's house flashing cards and she thought they were police badges. They were saying: 'We have to talk to Christy. This is big. He could end up in jail over this.' Kathryn's ma nearly had a heart attack. So, thinking these people were trying to do me some good, she gave them our address.

Next they're sitting outside my house with zoom lens cameras and knocking down the door. I had to jump over the back wall to get out of my house. I couldn't answer the door, because if I did they'd say, 'We've heard you're big into heroin blah blah blah,' and if I said no they'd print everything they'd said and just put a single line at the end saying I'd denied it. I had to get my brother to move in with me so he could answer the door.

Something the comedian Billy Connolly said a long time ago has always stuck with me. He said that he's been famous at two different levels. Early on he was famous and poor, and that was a nightmare. Then he was famous and rich and that was much better because he could use his wealth to build a wall around his house if he felt the need to keep out the press and other invasive people. When you're famous and poor you have no wall, and you're exposed to everything all the time. When the tabloid storm blew up I understood exactly what Billy Connolly meant, because at that point I had the fame – or the notoriety – but I didn't have the funds that go with that fame. Living in our ordinary house in Finglas, myself, Kathryn and baby Kiera had no protection against this extreme harassment. We were under siege night and day, and they were like a pack of wolves.

The Tabloid Crucifixion of Christy Dignam: Day Four

'CHRISTY SMOKED HEROIN IN FRONT OF HIS BABY CIARA [SIC], THEN HE SAID ... "THIS IS GOOD STUFF"'

The house in Kilmaroney Close, Donaghmede, was like any other suburban semi. But to sacked Aslan singer Christy Dignam it was a drugs haven where he could blow his mind. The rock star – the idol of thousands of youngsters – smoked heroin ... as his two-and-a-half-year-old daughter Ciara [sic] innocently looked on.

Irish Star, 10 September 1988

There was nothing in *The Star* on the third day of our ordeal, but there was loads of shit going on and the house was still surrounded.

The morning of day four arrived and it looked quiet out front, so I ran over to the shop across the road from my house. Before that, every time I'd go in it would be, 'Howaya, Christy!' and I'd get a real warm welcome from the shopkeepers and the customers. Until this Saturday, day four, I go in and they're all looking at me like I'm a piece of shit.

I looked down at the newspapers on the floor and the headline on *The Star* was 'CHRISTY SMOKED HEROIN IN FRONT OF HIS BABY' in huge letters. My knees nearly buckled under me. I grabbed the paper, ran back into the house and read it. They used a photo they'd taken months earlier of me, Kathryn and Kiera all sitting together on the couch. *The Star* had taken it for a 'family man of rock'-type soft-focus feature. But now they were reusing these family shots with little pull-outs of text saying things like: 'Christy blew rings of heroin smoke into little Kiera's face'.

Horrible. Horrible. The lies they told were sickening. So I sued them.

My case against *The Star* would take months to get to court. In the meantime I had more immediate problems to deal with. I was cut adrift with incredible speed by all these people who the week before pretended to be my best friends. One of the most hurtful fair-weather friends who cold-shouldered me the moment it happened was a well-known radio and TV personality who'd hitched himself to the Aslan bandwagon. I used to do coke with him and Gerry Ryan out in RTÉ, putting the lines out on the desk in the studio between shows. What a hypocrite!

It was a repeat – except on an individual level – of when all the record companies ran a mile after CBS turned us down. It was like I had a dose of the plague: 'Get away from that fucker!' As I've said, the only salvation in the whole thing was that the Irish media – the print media – generally stood behind me. They were totally against this character assassination by *The Star*, because that sort of thing had never happened in Ireland before, and it wasn't Irish journalism.

Then, when the dust had settled a bit, stories started coming out of the Aslan camp that I wouldn't be a huge loss because I hadn't been pulling my weight. They said at the time that I was contributing nothing, and in fairness I wasn't involved in the writing anymore and I was turning up late for rehearsals. I later came to accept that what they were saying was mostly true but at the time all I felt was insult being piled on injury.

I think at the time Joe fancied himself as a bit of a singer. I think Joe today would admit that much himself, and that's what happened when they gave up on Eamo Doyle. They dropped the Aslan name and formed Precious Stones, with Joe as their frontman. I think Joe would now agree that it was only when he started fronting the Precious Stones that he realised there's a big difference between getting out there and singing, and putting on a performance.

31

A Day in Court

I sued *The Star* for printing lies about me, and when we got to court their solicitor stood up and started describing this really nasty bloke and saying things like, 'This man is a self-confessed heroin addict and blah blah blah,' and I'm sitting there thinking, holy fuck, he's talking about *me*. If I was the judge, *I'd* have put that fucker he's talking about in jail – but it was *me* he was talking about!

When they ran the three stories over four days I immediately went to a solicitor and said, 'I'm not having this.' I wanted an apology in the paper that my ma would be able to show the neighbours and say it wasn't true. She'd been so proud just a few weeks earlier going to the big outdoor city centre show in a limo. Then, so quickly, she was so shamed that she didn't want to go out her front door. In court the lawyer for *The Star* started this character assassination of me, and then their senior counsel asked for a recess. He went over to my barrister and they talked, and then we all went out into the hallway. They were over one side and I was on the other, and they came over and said, 'Right, we'll give you 5,000 pounds and that's the end of it.'

I said no. I said I also wanted a retraction. And I told

them I didn't want it on the inside back page, below the horse racing results. I wanted it in italics and I wanted it up the front.

They told me I couldn't have the front page because that had to be held for breaking news, like if someone important died. So all this was going back and forward. They were coming back saying that they'll place the retraction where they want to place it, and it won't be in italics, and I'm saying no, that's a deal breaker and so on. Then their offer to me went up to 11 grand, and then 25 grand, and that's where I made an eternal mistake. I said I didn't give a fuck about the money end of it; I just wanted the retraction. It never went above 25 grand after that. I fucked up. I shouldn't have said that.

The result was that they gave me all the conditions I asked for on the retraction, but it was on the inside. It was in italics, so it stood out on the page, and in it they apologised and said what they had published about me wasn't true.

Up to this point it had taken probably eighteen months to get to court, and I had my solicitor on a retainer. I used to give him 80 pounds every month, so I had spent thousands of pounds before getting to court. I was awarded 25 grand plus costs, but when the money came through six months after the court case, I was handed a lot less. So I said to the solicitor, 'Hold on, I got awarded 25 grand.'

'Ah no, your costs came out of that.'

'But I was awarded costs.'

'Ah, that's only court costs.'

There were other costs outside of the court costs. Like, we had a private investigator checking things.

I was shocked and dismayed.

After my case against *The Star* was settled, we went to a pub beside the Four Courts. In the pub my solicitor told me that if I stepped out of line so much as an inch from now on I would be crucified. He said I had to be extremely careful of everything I did from now on.

32

The Damage Done

I was so ashamed and embarrassed by what happened that for a long time afterwards I distanced myself from my folks, from by brothers and sisters, from my family, from all of them. My folks were always cool about all that stuff about the break-up of the band, and the bust, and the tabloid muck. It was only when the story of my sex abuse came out shortly afterwards that my da said, 'You shouldn't be talking about that. Things like that happen to everybody. You just forget about it.'

I didn't understand his attitude until years later when I learned for the first time about the abuse he'd suffered from the Christian Brothers at Artane Industrial School in Dublin. I've told earlier about how my da's father died and the priest refused to come to the house because there was no money to pay him. Shortly after his father died, my da was put into Artane because the family's breadwinner was gone. At that time you could get locked up in an industrial school for a lot less than mitching from school or for misbehaving. There were these state inspectors going around, and if they decided that a family was too big and the parents couldn't take care of them all, they'd take two or three of the kids out of the home and throw them into places like Artane, which were run with sheer brutality.

My da never talked about that to anybody until the government set up a redress commission for victims of institutional abuse in 2002. He decided he'd go before the commission and give his account of what happened to him. My da was one of nearly 17,000 children abused under state care who lived long enough to tell their stories and demand redress. It was only then, maybe fifty years after he'd left Artane, that my da confided in my brother, Brian, who was then working for a health authority. He asked Brian to go with him to the redress commission to help him present his case. But even to this day my da thinks that Brian is the only one who knows about what happened to him. He's never discussed it with any other family member.

My friend Mike Hickey comes with me when I go up to see my da every Saturday. Mike's father was in Artane Industrial School at around the same time, and the two of us will sit there, in front of my da, and discuss the horrors that went on in Artane. And my da will sit there and listen and there will be not a single word out of him about ever being in the place.

When it comes to healing wounds, many people believe that some things are best left unsaid. I don't know about that. I have this belief that there's two states – there's darkness and there's light – and in my experience anything I've ever brought into the light has been of benefit to me, and anything I've kept in the dark has been detrimental to me. That might not be a way that suits everyone, but that is my experience.

For example, one of the twelve steps to recovery in NA

(Narcotics Anonymous) is that we make amends to those we've hurt in the past. So, say for example I ripped someone off while I was using heroin. Say I took 100 quid out of someone's wallet. I'd go back to that person, repay them the 100 quid, say I'm sorry and hope that they would accept my making amends. You have to make that effort, otherwise you're left carrying that baggage around and it's detrimental to your recovery. But the key thing is that you have to make amends without hurting other people or hurting yourself. For example, a bloke isn't going to make any amends to his bird by saying, 'Listen, love, while we were broke up I was riding everything that walked. I really love you. I'd never do it in a sober mind, but I did do it and I'm sorry.' That's not going to heal anybody. That's just going to do more damage.

There are exceptions to every rule and you have to make that call on each case as it comes up. If you think something is better left in the dark, keep it in the dark.

33

No Thanks, Marillion,
Yes Please, Terence Trent

SFX, DUBLIN, 7 BANDS ON THE UP PRESENTS
SOMETHING HAPPENS, CHRISTY DIGNAM, MISSING
LINK

If there had been a fatted calf in the SFX tonight it would
surely have been slain for the return of Christy Dignam, *The
Star's* Prodigal Son. Exhibiting a vitality usually reserved for
the Gods or the insane, Christy led his many fans, old and
new, hand-in-hand through most of Aslan's debut album
and his recent solo material. There was a genuine sense of
rejoicing here which was best displayed on the closing 'This
Is', with the crowd singing out the fitting refrain 'Everybody
hits you/Everybody knocks you down' long after Christy
had left the stage.

'Return of the Prodigal Son', *Hot Press*, May 1989

While I was still in no man's land after the band split and
the tabloid mauling, I got a call to say that Marillion were
looking for a new singer. Their frontman Fish had left the
band and they were auditioning for a replacement. EMI rang
me and asked, would I audition for Marillion? I told them

thanks, but there was no way I was going to stand in a queue of hopefuls with ten minutes in an audition to prove myself. I told them to tell Marillion to go out and buy a copy of *Feel No Shame*, and if they were interested they could get back to me.

They were interested. I went over to England and I spent a weekend rehearsing with the band. They were into it but I wasn't. For one thing, I was twenty-eight and they would have all been around forty. Plus I hated the music. It was sub-Genesis prog rock and I wasn't into it at all. They were all nice people, but it wasn't my bag. The album they wanted me to sing on was called *Season's End*, and when it came out a few months later it went straight into the Top 10 in the UK.

Did I consider doing the Marillion gig for a while, just to get money in the bank? Maybe if that opportunity had come up now, when I'm a lot older, I might have viewed it as a means of making a good living for a year or so. I might take that view today because I'm more of a professional musician now. But back then I still had a dream, and although Aslan were split up I never thought the split was cast in iron. It was only a few months since the band had broken up and I still thought we might get back together. It was only after a year or two had passed that I put that possibility out of my mind.

An opportunity opened up to strike out on my own. Terence Trent D'Arby was in Ireland doing *Neither Fish nor Flesh*, his follow-up to *Introducing the Hardline According to . . .*, which had been a worldwide smash. He'd block-booked Windmill Lane Studios on Dublin's quays for a lengthy period. Then his girlfriend in London had a baby, so Terence went off to be with her and his firstborn child. Tim Martin was engineering the album. He'd worked with us on the *Feel No Shame* album and he was the one who gave me Phil Lynott's leather jacket. I think Tim felt sorry for me after reading all the shit in the papers. He gave me a call and said Terence Trent D'Arby's studio was sitting there paid for, and I could use it. So I flew in there with some musician mates and we recorded 'One Man's Dream' over two and a half days. Then Oliver Walsh from the record label asked, 'What's on the B-side?' *Aah.*

We found ourselves with half a day left of Terence Trent D'Arby's studio time to write and record a B-side. So I told the guitarist Fred Malone to play three chords. He asked, 'What three chords?'

I said, 'Any three chords.'

They didn't work, so I told him to play another three chords, and another. We eventually got three chords I liked and we had our B-side – 'Chasing Shadows'. Eventually 'Chasing Shadows' was released as a single in its own right, and it got to number three in the Irish charts.

I decided to put together my own band to gig around the new single. I didn't want Cactus World News' drummer and In Tua Nua's bass player or any of these brilliant musicians from all the generic bands around Dublin. Instead I got together a bunch of young musicians who I liked as people, in the hope of putting together an organic band of mates, like Aslan had been. They were all lovely blokes, and we got a great reception from audiences, but the more we played together the more it hammered home how good Aslan had become and how much I'd lost when we'd split.

After all those years of playing together the members of Aslan had developed a kind of telepathy. When we played we knew what each other was thinking. But now, with the new band, I had to explain everything. I had to almost play out the drumbeat. It was too much. I tried to write songs for an album in a rehearsal space down by Croke Park and it just wasn't happening. I just couldn't get my head around it.

34

Introducing Conor Goff on Guitar

My new single is brilliant. It's the best single in the world today. 'Like A Child' sounds very American but it's got a lot more power than the Americans have. I know I'm a very good guitar player – probably one of the better guitar players in the country. Certainly in the top ten.

Conor Goff, *Hot Press*, 1987

One day around the time I realised my new band wasn't really up to scratch, I was in RTÉ and I ran into Neil Joyce, a medical doctor who was besotted with the musical scene. He was after putting a load of money into a big hair metal band called Conor Goff and the Crash, but they'd come to an end and Conor was over in the States trying to make a go of it on his own. Neil had this unexpected proposition. He asked if I'd be interested in putting a band together with Conor Goff. I knew Conor, and I knew the American metal music he played, and I thought it was shit, so I said I wasn't interested. But Neil assured me that Conor had changed his style. I gave it some thought and decided that maybe Conor might have some capability that he wasn't using, and maybe between us we could come up with something fresh.

Soon after that, Conor returned to Ireland from the States and we got a band together. And at that point I did something I'd swore I would never do – we got Cactus' drummer, In Tua Nua's bass player, Conor on guitar, me on vocals. It was exactly the sort of muso group I'd always detested. It didn't last. I let them go after we had a strong difference of opinion over whether people should be paid for playing a fundraising gig.

It was that era, around the beginning of the 1990s, when the *MTV Unplugged* sessions were all the rage, so myself and Conor started touring without a band. Financially it made a lot of sense at a time when rave culture was happening and the crowds for live acts were dwindling. I wrote a couple of good songs during that period, but nobody gave a fuck. People who were into Aslan just weren't into what I was doing with Conor Goff.

DIGNAM & GOFF ON THEIR UNLIKELY PARTNERSHIP

Dignam would have the most credibility. His saving grace always will be his svelte voice. Conor Goff, on the other hand, has always been given short shrift by the Irish rock intelligencia, being portrayed as a heavy-handed guitarist with little imagination. They're both well aware of how they're perceived by their critics. People have come up to Christy Dignam, drunk with ego and alcohol, and abused both him and his choice of musical partner.

'People hand you out advice,' says Dignam, 'and you wonder what the fuck are they doing with their own lives.'

In Dublin, 1990

Irish audiences just did not buy into me partnered with Conor Goff. Music is very tribal and we came from two tribes that were hostile to each other. Operating as an unplugged duo quickly ran out of steam on the small Irish gigging circuit, and one night we found ourselves sitting in Conor's car outside a venue in the Cork fishing village of Kinsale. We were counting the people going in so I could calculate if we would take enough money at the door to pay for the petrol back to Dublin. That's how bad it got. So we decided to try the States. We'd book, say, ten gigs along the east coast, around Yonkers, Queens, Bronx, Brooklyn, then up to Boston and down to Washington. It worked, and each time we went back over to the States the audiences were building.

There was a place called the Red Lion in Manhattan and I used to play there once a week on a Wednesday. My payment was a rent-free apartment above the venue. It was a brilliant set-up. The guy who owned the Red Lion used to bring the pub's staff on tuna-fishing expeditions to the coastal village of Montauk on the tip of Long Island, and myself and Conor were the house band for those work outings. This guy called Bud Prager Jnr turned up at our gig in Montauk one night. He told us that his dad, who was also called Bud Prager, managed Ben E. King, Foreigner, Bad Company, Megadeth and other big acts. He asked if we'd like to meet him. So we met Bud Prager Snr and he was mad into what we were doing.

In no time, Bud Snr negotiated a five-album deal for us with Epic Records. We were on the verge of signing when some issues came up between myself and Conor, which made me question whether I wanted to sign any legal documents that would tie me into a partnership with him for years to come. Conor would be bringing baggage into that partnership which I wasn't sure I wanted to share.

35

New Game, New Rules, Press Restart

I was still living in New York at the time I started having serious doubts about planning any future with Conor, and we were halfway into a two-month tour of the States when I came back to do an Aslan once-off outdoor show in Finglas. It was now five years after the split and we had run into each other once or twice. At one point I was doing a gig in the Baggot Inn with Conor Goff when Tony turned up in the audience. He jumped up on stage and did a couple of songs. That was the first little piece of bridge-building. A while after that I ran into the rest of them at Club 92 in Leopardstown. We were back talking, sort of. Before that, if we'd seen each other on the street we'd have been screaming abuse at each other. At its worst it was really bitter.

By 1993 a lot of the bitterness had faded and we were back talking on good terms. There was a promoter called Robbie Foy who used to put on a big free open-air show each year for the Finglas Festival in a place called the Janelle Centre. We played it every year before the split as a thank you to our local fans. After the band broke up the annual festival gig stopped for me and the others, but every year Robbie would ask us if we'd get back together just for a once-off for the kids in Finglas.

For the first couple of years I'd tell him no way, I wouldn't have anything to do with those scumbags. And they'd be saying the same about me. Then, maybe the third year Robbie asked, I'd say, 'Okay, I'll do it if they'll do it, but just as a once-off.' But they wouldn't do it. And the next year they'd want to do it but I'd refuse to get involved. That's the way it went on. Then 1993 came around and Robbie came to us and said, 'Look, I'm losing my sponsorship, but the sponsors will stay on board if Aslan play.' And it was a big deal for Finglas. It was the main event of the festival, which was the only proper community gathering Finglas had at the time. So this time when Robbie came asking, we decided we'd do it as a once-off to save his sponsorship.

I came back from New York and we had two weeks' rehearsal time. In the first week we rehearsed the set for the show, which was more or less *Feel No Shame* and one or two songs that would have been on the second album. It went so well that after a week we had the set worked out, and we had really nothing left to do, so we decided to try some new stuff, and that's where 'Crazy World' came about, along with a few other pieces. I came up with a song called 'This Time', which would eventually appear on the *Goodbye Charlie Moonhead* album.

I was surprised at how easy, how seamless, the reconnection was in an artistic sense. It was great to be back with a band again. My heart was never in the Conor Goff thing. It was something I had to do to pay the bills, and I was doing all the writing, but the writing wasn't coming easy. I couldn't play an instrument, so I needed musicians to write with, to bounce off. Conor was no good for that. Back with Joe and Tony, we just found that connection straight away. The new songs went so well that we sat down and said to each other, 'Will we give this another go?

We made that decision to start over, but once we decided to give it a go I was never, ever going to leave myself vulnerable the way I had the first time around. It was never going to be like that again. We laid down the ground rule that everybody in the band had their little idiosyncrasies and you either tolerated them or you could fuck off now. There was no saying sorry for what had happened five years in the past. A line was drawn in the sand. We didn't need to say anything. We're not a touchy-feely bunch. What happened happened. They did what they had to do at the time, and I knew I'd wronged them. We weren't going to get into all that shit again. That's the way it kicked off for the second part of the Aslan story.

It wasn't all plain sailing of course. We'd been back together a while and I was after getting back into the drugs. An Emotional Fish had long parted company and their singer Gerry Fish was around the band a bit. I said to the others, 'I hope you're not thinking of replacing me with Gerry Fish.' And Billy said, 'Ah no, we tried that before and it didn't work.'

That came as a jolt to me. I'd come back into the band thinking that we were all united again, that we were all going for this together again. I thought this was a fresh start and we were moving forward. But when Billy said that, it struck me that they weren't doing it for the love of getting back together this tight little gang we'd once had; it was just that fiscally this was the best option to take. That knocked me for six at the time, and it took me a while to get over that realisation. The others had each other to bounce off, but for a while after I was back I felt isolated within the group. I felt like a bit of an outsider, and that reinforced my insecurities. It took a while to get over that, but I did and we did, and we've left all that long in the past.

The last gig Dignam & Goff did was in Cumiskey's of Cabra, and I thought it would be good to finish it off with a party back in my gaff, which was quite close to the venue. Conor said he was just going to pack away his stuff and he'd see me there in ten minutes. That was more than a quarter of a century ago and I've not laid eyes on him from that day to this.

The following summer I was back in New York, but this time with Aslan. It was 1994 and the World Cup Finals were being held over there and all of Ireland seemed to be in New York for Ireland's opening game against Italy. I hooked up with some of the heads from my time living over the Red Lion, who I hadn't seen in a while. One of them had run into Conor recently and he said to me, 'Hey, man, is he pissed with *you*!'

I said, 'What?' As far as I was concerned the split with Conor had been a mutual thing, and he'd said he was okay with it, but he clearly wasn't.

The real purpose of that trip to the States was to try to reconnect with Bud Prager Snr. My thinking was that since Prager and Epic Records had really liked Dignam & Goff, they were going to *love* Aslan because we were so much better. So we did a gig for Prager in Tramps of New York. It's a top Manhattan venue where they've had Bob Dylan, Springsteen, Prince, Chuck Berry and everyone who's anyone. We played our set and, after the show, Prager said to us, 'Can you do another show tomorrow but this time do it unplugged?'

We said, 'We're not an acoustic band. What you've just seen is what we are.'

And the response to that was we could just fuck off.

In Ireland we had what you'd call street credibility. Over in America that meant fuck all.

36

Fear and Loathing in Dublin City

I knew that Aslan had conquered Ireland on their second time around when I heard my neighbour tunelessly strum 'Crazy World', the band's phenomenally successful comeback single. But although the single has spent three months in the charts the band aren't crazy about the song. Frontman Christy Dignam explains: 'I've released better songs than "Crazy World" that never did shit, but for some reason it just tapped into something. Sometimes when you release a song it taps into the psyche of the nation.'

Mick Heaney, In Dublin, 1993

'Crazy World' was the hit of the summer in Ireland that year, so we went straight into the studio to record a batch of new songs. The reason we called our reunion album, *Goodbye Charlie Moonhead*, was to say goodbye to a certain attitude of negativity that was all around. Charlie Moonhead was a drug dealer from Ballymun who would not see any good in us trying to make something of ourselves. When we were struggling for recognition, we'd turn up at Tony's place in the Ballymun Flats in the mornings and load up a couple of supermarket trolleys with amps and gear, and then wheel them towards the pigsty at the airport. We'd be pushing them past Charlie Moonhead's dealing patch and he'd be roaring out: 'So, yez think yiz are gonna be rock stars. Yez fuckin' eejits!'

And we're thinking, why have that attitude? You're selling drugs, for fuck's sake. We're trying to do something. We wanted people from Finglas and Ballymun to be proud of us. That was important to us. From the time I started sending off job applications, I'd just put my address as the postal code Dublin 11. I'd leave out the Finglas West part, because as soon as any prospective employer saw Finglas on your application, that was it, there was no job for you there. So you grew up with all that prejudice, and it still exists. I wanted something good to come out of Finglas, something that people could be proud of. I was very staunch on that.

Having said that, I never felt that I represented Finglas. I represented a very small proportion of the people who grew up in Finglas. I'd like to represent them all, but I'm just one person and I've my own life to live too. I never had to endure the absolute poverty of an awful lot of people in Finglas.

The launch of the *Goodbye Charlie Moonhead* album was great fun. We sent out invites to all the music journalists, and on the invitations it said to bring your passport. They all got very excited about this. We picked them all up in a double-decker bus on the south side of town and we headed across the Liffey and out north along the route to Dublin Airport. They were convinced they were off to somewhere exotic, until we got to Ballymun and the bus pulled up outside The Towers pub where I'd played my first-ever gig with Joe's outfit Electron all those years before. We played the songs from the new album and everyone had a laugh, then we all headed back into town to continue the party.

For me personally, the party mood was not to last too long after the band reformed. I started using gear again, and then a figure turned up from my past who I'd thought was out of my life forever. It was Paschal Boland, the dealer whose flat I'd been in when the bust took place and my life was torn to pieces.

After the Clonliffe bust, Paschal Boland racked up more charges for dealing. He was caught in other raids, including one where he tried to bring gear in through Dublin Airport. So when it came to his day in court he got nine years for all the charges combined. He went away in 1988, and now, in the mid-'90s, he was out.

He put the word out through the grapevine that he was looking for 50 grand from me. I couldn't believe this, and decided it would be best to avoid him, but friends of his were coming up to me saying he wanted to see me, and that he wanted this and he wanted that. So I ended up ringing him and he said to me, 'I did time for you.'

As if he did nine years behind bars for me!

I'm sure that while he was sitting there in prison he was hearing 'Crazy World' on the radio every five minutes and he was thinking there was Christy Dignam out there, earning millions like Elton John. I have no doubt that people were coming along filling his head with this notion – his visitors and other prisoners. While he was in jail I'd been buying him runners and tracksuits and lodging money into his prison scrapbook for cigarettes and small things, just to keep him sweet. So when he gets out, and he comes to me looking for money, I was shocked and shaken. When he was living the high life before he got locked up, he used to have all these fancy cars. He had a high-performance Sierra Cosworth, which was built for motorsport and was the dog's bollocks at the time. He had classic Model-T Fords. He had powerful motorbikes. Then, when he was locked up after his conviction, all his so-called friends sold off all that stuff. His friends took everything of his that wasn't nailed down, but when he came out of jail he wasn't looking for any of them, only me!

Having someone like that on your trail is scary. He was a dangerous heavy. At the time of his jailing he practically ran the heroin trade on the north side of Dublin. But what happened to him – what always happens – is that you come out of jail thinking you're still cock of the walk but in the years you've been inside a new crew has come in and taken over. So here's this yesterday's man looking for 50 grand off me to get himself on his feet again.

This is going on and on for maybe three years. I'm ducking and diving, trying to stay out of his way, and all the time I'm living in absolute terror because he's putting out all these threats to me. What you have to understand is that he was a drug dealer and I was a heroin addict, because I was back active then. So I'm desperately trying to avoid him but I'm in the same world as him. This is a world where people are setting other people up all the time to get snatched or to get shot. The pressure of trying to just exist and avoid him was exhausting.

I was living in this state of terror and exhaustion, living

under all these threats. It seemed that things couldn't get any worse, and then they did. They got a lot worse. Paschal got this deranged maniac involved. He was known as Psycho and there was no one more feared in Dublin. I arrived home one day and Kathryn told me that this guy Peter had knocked at the house wanting to see me. The caller had left a card with just the name Peter printed on it and a phone number. I didn't know who it was, so I did nothing. Then the same bloke called up again when I wasn't there. When he was walking back out the drive, Kathryn looked out the window and saw that waiting for him in the car was Paschal Boland.

This time I called the number on the card. A bloke answered and I said, 'Hello, Peter, this is Christy Dignam.'

He said, 'I want to see you.'

I asked him, 'What's it about?'

He said, 'I'll fuckin' tell you what it's about when I see you.'

So I said, 'C'mere, you. Who the fuck do you think you are? Go fuck yourself!'

I hung up. Now, if I'd known who I was talking to, it would have been a different conversation.

That same day I went up to Finglas to see my mate Penner, Michael Penrose, who knew Paschal. I asked Penner, 'Who does Paschal Boland know that has red hair, a stocky little fucker, drives a Honda Civic?'

Penner told me: 'That's PJ Judge. Psycho.'

When I heard I nearly shat myself. I swear to God. Because that man was a fucking animal. And I'm thinking, oh, Jaysus Christ, what have I done, 'cos I'm after tearing the fucking liver out of this fucker on the phone. So this is all going on and I find out that Boland owed money to Psycho and told him, 'Dignam has money belonging to me.' So the plan was that they'd get the money off me and Paschal Boland could pay Psycho.

And now I'd told Psycho to go fuck himself. I'd been living in fear of Paschal for three years, but this was a different level of sheer terror. I went into hiding. If a knock came to the door I was looking out the cracks. Then, only two or three weeks later, I stopped at a petrol station on the way from a gig late on a Saturday night, and they had the next morning's Sunday papers on the counter. I picked up the *Sunday World* and the front-page headline said: 'PJ JUDGE ASSASSINATED IN FINGLAS'. I know it's a horrible thing to say, but a weight just lifted off me and I said, 'Thanks be to Jaysus for that!'

When Paschal got Psycho involved, my problems escalated from the Championship to the Premiership. The threat and the terror went from the second division to the highest level. With Judge gone, things went back to the second level. I still had Paschal Boland to deal with, and I was still in deep, deep trouble. I was hearing stories that while Paschal had been in prison, the gang known as the Westies were running all the drugs in Blanchardstown, which is where Paschal lived, and which used to be his old patch. Paschal came out and tried to set up again, but the Westies told him it wasn't going to happen. His day was gone. I was happy to hear this, because it meant that Paschal was losing his power, but he was still dangerous, and he was still very dangerous to me.

Then a young fella told me that that Boland was planning to lift my daughter Kiera off the street and get his money that way. Kiera was around the age of eight or nine at the time. That was the end of the ducking and diving. I got Paschal's phone number, rang him, and arranged to meet him at the Slipper pub in Ballymun. He would have been out of jail three years at this time, but I hadn't seen him since he got out. Walking into that place I was absolutely terrified. He was sitting at the bar waiting for me. He was about five-ten, stocky, skinhead – a thug.

I said to him, 'Look, Paschal, I've lived in terror of you for the past three years. Whatever you're saying out there, you know in your heart that I've done nothing on you. You know that I looked after you when you were inside. I brought you runners and tracksuits and I left money on your book while you were locked up. I was the only one who looked after you – nobody else did. I'm not a gangster. I'm a nobody, but I swear to God if you touch Kiera you'd better kill me stone dead because I'll come after you. I'll go to jail for you.'

He says back to me, 'Christy, you're losing it! I wasn't threatening anything. I'm just asking you to get a loan of money from the bank to set me back up. I'll invest it. Then when I make some money I'll pay you back.'

Pay me back. That was bullshit. But it gave me an out of that face-to-face, and I walked out of there telling him I'd try to get a loan from the bank.

The very next day he rang me, keeping the pressure on. I told him I'd tried to get a bank loan and they laughed at me.

He started coming the heavy again.

'I need that money. Try somewhere else. Try the credit union.'

So when he rang back the next day I told him I'd tried the credit union, and tried here, and tried there, but no one was going to lend me money.

I explained to him over and over that I hadn't a pot to piss in. I might have been earning a living but I had no money as such. No bank was going to give me a loan of even a small amount of money. There was no way I could raise 50 grand for him. So that was that, and I heard no more for a while. Then one day the same bloke who'd told me Boland was going to kidnap Kiera came up to me on the street.

'Ha, you must be sick, Dignam, you had to give Paschal Boland 30 grand!'

When the young fella said this to me I was going to argue with him. I was going to tell him I didn't give Boland a penny. Then it struck me that Boland obviously had to save face, and if that's the way he wants to do it, and if it means that's the end of it, then I don't give a fuck. So I just let it go at that. All these people thought I'd paid Paschal Boland 30 grand, which I hadn't, but that was the end of it.

As I've said, while Boland was out of circulation the Westies gang had taken over the heroin trade around Blanchardstown and Finglas. From what I gather, from what the folklore says, Boland started buying gear over in Ballyfermot, cutting it up, and selling it on the north side. The Westies told him that his old turf was their turf now, so fuck off! He wouldn't listen. He was getting out of his car in his driveway one night and he was shot dead. It was the Westies that killed him.

That was 1999, and that was my two tormentors gone, Paschal and Psycho. I know it's horrible to say it, but it was like a thorn taken out of my side. The relief was unbelievable. I actually felt bad about the fact I felt so good about it. It's not Christian, is it? But I had been terrorised by them.

Kathryn had been watching all this for the three years it was happening. This was the shit she was putting up with on a daily basis. She didn't know about the threat to kidnap Kiera, because I didn't tell her until much later. I didn't give her the details of what was happening but I told her that Paschal was threatening to kill me and he was looking for money. She knew all that, and it was going on right through Kiera's childhood years.

How did things ever get to such a sorry state? By increments. People look at a junkie sitting in a doorway on O'Connell Street today, and they think, how the fuck did you do this to yourself? But that junkie didn't wake up on a Tuesday morning, get dressed in his suit and tie for his great job in the bank, and then shoot up on the way to work and fall into a doorway. It took years to get to that doorway. As I've said, it happens by increments. Addiction is death by a thousand cuts. If myself and Kathryn had arrived back from Australia full of plans to get married and the next day we'd woken up to a psychopath banging on the door for money, that would probably have ended our relationship. We'd never have made it to the altar. But it didn't happen in one day; it happened very gradually over a long period of years.

Kathryn had a hairdresser's in Finglas, so she would have heard all the stories about me. She'd have been gradually building a picture of what was really happening. So then, when something serious happens, it doesn't seem like such a big deal, because in a way you've been prepared.

As for me, I gradually lost track of what was normal behaviour. One Sunday afternoon we went to Bray for a family day out. I was strung out. I told Kathryn I needed to go to the jacks. The men's public toilets were out of order, so I went into the ladies' jacks. There was a mirror in there and I stood in front of it so I could squeeze a vein in my neck to make it stand out, so I could inject into my neck. So I banged in the needle, and I was drawing out the blood – that's how you know you have the vein – and I was in the process of doing this when these two old women walk in on top of this scene. They gasped at me with a look of shock and horror on their faces that I can't begin to describe.

And what did I do? I said to them, 'Aw, don't look at me like that. I know it's not the nicest thing you've ever seen, but don't be overreacting like that.'

And I genuinely meant that. I rebuked them. I had lost it to the point that what was so deeply shocking for ordinary people was for me an everyday occurrence. What was there to get upset about? That's the mentality you get into.

And because I was becoming that person, for Kathryn to survive in that situation she almost had to build up the same walls against the outside world as I had. She had to build the same insulation between herself and normality. Otherwise she would be so horrified that she could never survive living with me. When things got really bad I was coming home covered in abscesses from injecting, and she would have to see me in that state. Again, it was gradual. It started off with one little bump, and then the bump got infected and I had to find another spot to inject, and then that got infected. And so on until I was covered with sores. Eventually it all just got too much for Kathryn, but we'll get to that shortly.

37

Everybody Hits You, Everybody Knocks You Down

The momentum created by the band's happy reunion and the success of the *Charlie Moonhead* album ran out of steam. Their record label, BMG, rejected their follow-up album and dropped the band. Dejected, Aslan begin playing small pub gigs in order to stay solvent as a band. At one show, violent scuffles erupted at the end of their set, which were broken up by the police as innocent gig-goers cowered under tables and the band retreated to their dressing room.

Aslan's Crazy World (official biography), 1997

As much as we might have normalised that sort of stuff – like playing that low-rent dive where the trouble broke out – we knew deep down that we shouldn't be there. It was a way of paying the rent at the time, but we knew in our hearts that we were letting ourselves down and that we were in a very bad place.

But we kept doing it, going back to playing venues we'd never have dreamed of playing a couple of years earlier. Life has taught me, and especially living with an addiction has taught me, that that's the human condition. You forget what used to be normal and you fall into a new normal.

We fell into this vicious cycle because we'd been with BMG Records, and we'd left six months free to tour Britain with the *Charlie Moonhead* album, which had done really well in Ireland. We were rehearsing for the tour and getting everything ready. The tour was to kick off at the end of July that year, and as we were coming into July we weren't hearing anything from the London office. BMG's Irish office weren't ringing us either. So I got really suspicious. I knew something wasn't right. We pushed BMG for tour details and were told that their head office in England had decided not to go with the album. They said there were no hits on the album. 'Crazy World' was on that album!

What had happened was that two blokes who'd been with Ensign were now running BMG in London. When they were with Ensign years earlier they'd turned us down and signed Sinéad O'Connor instead, so when they took over BMG that was that for us.

When BMG dropped us at such a crucial point, it sounded to me like they were saying 'Crazy World' was a big hit in Ireland only because the Irish were stupid. The stupid Irish made 'Crazy World' a hit because they don't know what a hit is. I felt an insult to my Irishness more than I did an insult to my abilities as a songwriter or a singer. So we were left with six months in front of us where we were supposed to be touring Britain, and now we had nothing to do. And we'd no money either.

But I'd been there before. When I was with Conor Goff I'd

played all these venues. I said to the others, 'Look, the cabaret label is only determined by what music you're playing, not where you're playing.' I was probably lying to myself, but we started playing bars.

I ran into one of our contemporary bands around that time and they said they were splitting up. I asked why they were ending it and they said it was because they'd lost their record deal.

I couldn't get my head around that concept. I put it to them that just because some bean counter in London had made a business decision about their band you've decided that your band now has no relevance, has nothing to say? Are you fucking mental? I told them they should believe in themselves and get their band back together. They never did.

And for us it's come to pass that we did believe in ourselves and we're still here all these years later. We've come out the other side. We stuck to it because we love what we do. We're not writing as much new stuff as we did back in the day, but we're still playing songs that we wrote back in the day.

We've come out the other side a strong unit. There's not the unconditional love there was in the early days, but you don't go through what we've been through without some scar tissue. The band were split up for five years, but either side of that we've been together thirty years, and we share a strong bond of trust. I've said earlier that we can never un-ring the bell on what happened, but the break-up was a long time ago and what I can say now with absolute truth is that I would not have taken this journey with anybody else. I would never say that I'd wished one of them wasn't in the band, and that Johnny so-and-so had been in the band instead. Nobody could have been replaced.

We all fill different roles in the band, on and off the stage, and we all have complete trust in the others to fulfil their roles. Alan is very steady and mathematical in his thinking; he has a precision that suits being a drummer. There's not a great deal of flamboyance to his character, but if everyone was flamboyant we'd drive each other mad. Alan's character makes him ideal to take care of all the band's finances. He does the accounts and files the taxes because he's completely trustworthy, reliable, and as honest as the day is long.

Joe is meticulous in everything he does. He's almost OCD, an obsessive-compulsive character. I've mentioned his fixation with putting together the fiddly little toys from Kinder Eggs, but that's just one example. He'd have about 100 of the little thingamajigs on the dashboard of the car. He also assembles and flies model planes. He's mad into anything to do with modelling, and when he makes a model aeroplane it's like it's after coming straight out of the factory. Joe brings his meticulous ways about everything to the band. When we're writing songs I'll sing a melody, and often, once I get a melody I like, I'll just keep repeating it throughout the verse. But then Joe will come in with his ear for fine detail. He's the one in the band with the most musical ability. He'll bring in minor chords and other subtle changes to melodies.

There are times when Joe's obsessive-compulsive side can get a bit weird. He came into my hotel room one time and it was in the usual state. My bag was open on the floor.

All my stuff was strewn across the bed. Whatever clothes I'd been wearing the night before were all over the floor, along with the bath towels and everything else. Then we went from my room into Joe's room. We were staying in this hotel for just one night but Joe had taken out all his clothes, ironed them and put them neatly into the drawers and closet. Unbelievable, but that's Joe.

Billy is the joker in the pack. He brings the light-heartedness and he has a gift for defusing tense or uncomfortable situations. Having said that, Billy is very black and white. He's either for you or against you in any given situation and never the twain shall meet. There's no grey areas with Billy.

I can be very self-conscious doing interviews or when the band has to do meet-and-greet stuff. If we're meeting some Lord Mayor or some business bigwig, I'll turn up and try to do as little as I can. Billy will come in and talk to them like they're all best mates. Nowadays Billy does most of the interviews because I'm just interviewed out. When I do an interview these days it's 'How's the cancer?' and 'What's it like being on drugs?' Drugs and cancer. Cancer and drugs. For fuck's sake, give me a break! I've lived for more than half a century. I've done more than take drugs. Because of that, I leave most of the interviews to Billy, and he's the perfect pro for the job.

I've mentioned earlier about when I was in an emotionally fragile state, and I broke down singing, 'How can I protect you?' to Kathryn, who was watching from the audience. I couldn't go on. I had to get off the stage. In that moment of crisis and meltdown I was able to look at Billy and give him the nod, and he knew instinctively to jump in and take the reins. That's one example of what he does for the band in a thousand different ways.

In 2008 Tony McGuinness left the band he'd joined more than a quarter of a century earlier when we were still called Meelah XVIII. Tony was brilliant while he was with us. I initially got him in because he had a great haircut. Through the early years he was the fashion man, the flash dresser, the band's style icon, but he was also a great bass player and a gifted songwriter. Myself, Joe and Tony were the band's main songwriters, although most of the songs on our last album with Tony, *For Some Strange Reason*, were written by him. It didn't end well with Tony and this isn't the place to go into all that. All I can say is that I didn't want it to end the way it did. There is still some lingering bitterness and that's a shame, because the time we did spend together were great years.

That night of the riot when we had to take cover in the dressing room was one of the lowest points of all those years, but there was an upside to touring the pub circuit. We were playing pub gigs from Cork to Donegal, and what we found was that the people there really appreciated the fact we were coming to those little towns. We were building from the ground up again. That encouraged us to aim higher and we booked a show in Vicar Street. It sold out really quick, and then we added another, and another, until we were playing five nights in Vicar Street.

Denis Desmond of MCD Promotions was handling our bookings and we asked Denis for 40 grand to record the Vicar Street shows for a live album. He dug up the sales figures for the biggest-selling live album in Ireland the previous year – ... *There and Then* by Oasis. He told us that a live album by us would probably sell three-quarters of that figure, and there was no way he was spending 40 grand for that return. But we believed it could do much better than that and we decided to finance it ourselves. So we put our own money into it and it was huge, and that brought the touring back up to another level again. In Christmas week that year, 1999, we drew 9,000 people to a sold out Point Depot.

But even playing the Point I never felt it was a huge jump from the pub circuit a year earlier to there. And I never felt it was a huge comedown in the times after that when we dropped down a level. In the life cycle of a band that's been on the go as long as Aslan, there are always going to be times when you're up and times when you're down – and there *were* times when it got bad again. I never felt embarrassed if things weren't going well. As far as I was concerned, for those people who came to any gig, it was still one of the best gigs they were ever at. I knew there was quality to what we were doing. I still had that belief that it was what you played, not where you played, that determined whether you were or were not a cabaret band. When we started doing it, other name bands were poo-pooing us because we were playing these cabaret-type venues, and then two years later they were ringing us asking, 'Can you give us the number of such-and-such a place?'

We stuck with it and it paid off when we went to Australia in the summer of 2000 and found that we could still draw big crowds. In Sydney we'd be playing to 2,000 people. We were drawing big crowds in Brisbane, Perth, Canberra, everywhere we went. The first time we toured Australia the audiences would have been mainly first-generation Irish emigrants. That was the case whenever we went to any country for the first time – America, Britain, France, Germany. But the Irish would bring along a mate from the host country, and then the next time we'd play there the mate would bring along five of their mates. It built up over the return visits so that we were playing to cosmopolitan Australian audiences.

There was a period, when I was messing around with drugs again, where Joe wasn't interested in writing new material anymore. He was just doing the bare minimum. Tony by then had become the main songwriter. But then, when Tony left the band, Joe started coming up with fresh riffs and ideas again. So there are times when people's enthusiasm wanes or picks up, but I don't think there's ever been a time when any of us has thought this is a really horrible existence but I'll keep doing it for the money.

38

Pitch Perfect with Sinéad

We were re-energised by touring Australia to full houses at the start of the millennium, and when we got back we were full of ideas for new songs. We gathered them together for an album called *Waiting for This Madness to End*. One of the songs we wrote for the album was called 'She's So Beautiful'. It's a lovely song and we thought of Sinéad O'Connor to provide some vocals. I had a bit of a connection with Sinéad because we both went to the same singing teacher, Frank Merriman. I did a charity gig with her, and we talked about doing something together, but nothing happened for ages. Then we wrote 'Up In Arms', this time with Sinéad specifically in mind. Sinéad was in great demand and she didn't have a lot of spare time, so we decided we'd work out all the arrangements and lay down the backing tracks so that all she had to do when she arrived was to sing. When she got to the studio we told her to do this and this, and she did exactly what we asked her to do. We were delighted at how well it went. We got everything finished very quickly as planned, and we said, 'That's great, Sinéad, thanks very much.'

She said okay, but could she just go back in and do one more take? She told us to just press play and let her ad lib over the music. We pressed play and watched her ad lib, and when she was finished we threw out everything we had and kept just the ad lib. It was perfect, far better than how we'd imagined it could be. Sinéad is an amazing singer. There is no one like her in the world. She's into music pure and simple, not all the showbiz trappings. On a personal level she can be hard to deal with. Most people have this sensor in their brain that rationalises what you're going to do, that looks at the repercussions of what you're going to do and decides whether this is the wise thing to do or not – she doesn't have that. She has no filter at all.

I look at Sinéad and all the problems she's had in her life, and part of me feels that I know why she ended up where she's at. She is too pure a soul to live in the world of rock'n'roll. Her soul is too pure. She has too much integrity. The world of rock'n'roll forces you to swallow your integrity through a million compromises, and if you resist that you pay a price for it. I look at one of Ireland's biggest butter-wouldn't-melt teen idols, who I won't name, and I see how he's broadened that out to become a Mister Showbiz. To achieve his level of sustained success you need to have that ruthless, don't-give-a-fuck-who-I-stamp-on attitude, and he has that in spades. I'll take Sinéad over his type every time.

39

They Say You're Jinxed

'PASSENGER PLANE SKIDS OFF SLIGO RUNWAY'

An investigation is underway in Sligo into how an aircraft carrying 40 people skidded off a runway and tilted into the sea. The incident happened as the aircraft landed during heavy rain. A member of the rock band Aslan, who were among the passengers on the Euroceltic Airways flight, described it as a 'very, very frightening experience'.

Irish Times, 4 November 2002

In the early part of the new millennium we were gigging extensively around Ireland and England, so we were doing a lot of flying. One stormy winter day we were flying into the airport at Strand Hill in Sligo, which is right on the beach. Myself and Billy were sitting right over the wing of the plane. It was a Fokker F50 propeller job, with maybe forty or fifty seats. When they were handing out the safety instructions, we got a special set because in a crisis we'd be in charge of opening the emergency door. The hostess was explaining what to do and we were going, 'Yeah, yeah, yeah', paying no attention.

It was a real rocky flight with heavy turbulence. Billy

was doing his Scotty impression from *Star Trek*: 'It's no use, Captain, I can nae hold her. She's breaking up!' On a normal landing the plane will touch down on its back wheels first and then the front comes down. On a normal flight you come through the clouds and the runway is a mile below you. We came through the clouds and the runway was just yards beneath us and the nose was pointing downwards instead of the tail of the plane.

The plane hit the runway and the instant it struck the ground the wheels exploded and the tyres started rattling around the rim. No more Scotty jokes. We snapped into a different headspace: this is fucking serious!

We reached the end of the runway but the plane kept on going, skating over a grass verge at high speed. We were skidding towards a low cliff and below that the Atlantic Ocean. The pilot veered the plane to one side and I remember looking out of the window at this huge burst tyre rattling around the rim and thinking, this is not a car we're in!

The plane is pissing along the grass verge on the side of the runway and all this muck is flying up and all I can do is look at it and think, Holy fuck! And then we've passed the end of the runway but we're still going and then *BUMP!* We've gone over the cliff and we're in the ocean and the nose of the plane is underwater and the tail is sticking up. When we'd hit the ground it was as if in a nanosecond everybody accepted that we were going to die. That moment of peaceful acceptance was really weird. When we finally came to a halt there was an eerie hush of total silence, and then pande-monium broke out. Everyone was screaming and all these oul wans start attacking me and Billy, screeching to get them out of the emergency exit.

Now everything was on a slant and me and Billy were standing on the backs of the seats trying to open the emergency door. And the hostess was crawling up the slant of the aisle towards us shouting, 'No, no, no!' I don't know who designed the Fokker 50 but they deserve a good kick in the hole. The propeller was located right outside the emergency door and it was still rotating at speed, so if we'd opened the door, anyone who jumped out would have been sliced to bits! If that plane was on fire and it was a choice between the flames and the propeller – what do you do? Eventually the propeller stopped moving, but even if you jumped then you'd be jumping into the Atlantic Ocean.

So we waited, stuck, and the next minute a Hiace van speeds up from the terminal with what looked like a window cleaner's ladder on the roof. The rescue crew jumped out and put this aluminum ladder up to the passenger door at the back of the plane. This had all taken so long there was no panic anymore and we were able to disembark in an orderly fashion down the ladder, but that still took twenty minutes. If that plane was on fire we'd all be dead. If the whole plane had gone into the water we'd all be dead.

First thing I did was ring Kathryn: 'Kathryn! We've been in a plane crash! I'm standing in the middle of the runway now.' She thought I was winding her up.

They brought us into the terminal and gave us Lucozade, Coke, a cup of tea, whatever. We got ourselves together and headed on to the venue for that night's show. Straightaway the crash-landing was all over the radio and television tea-time news. The band and crew always go out for something to eat before a gig, so we were having our meal when this crowd of oul wans arrived in from a coach tour. They recognised us straight off from the six o'clock news and this little woman comes over to me with her lottery ticket and says, 'You wouldn't touch that for me, son, would you? You're very lucky, very lucky.'

About a month later we were flying from Manchester to Glasgow, and about twenty minutes into the flight the captain announced there was a problem with the plane. Nothing serious, but we had to turn back. We turned around and, as we were approaching to land at Manchester, I could see that the runway was lined with fire engines and ambulances. From what I heard later, the flight computer broke down and the pilots had to fly by wire, manually, which they don't do anymore.

So I'm going, Holy Jaysus, this is not happening again! The same week that we crash-landed in Sligo, two other Fokkers came down. An F50 crashed in Luxembourg, with only two survivors, then days later an F27 smashed into Manila Bay, killing nineteen. It seemed we'd been very lucky.

We touched down safely in Manchester and the airline stuck us in the VIP lounge while they got a replacement plane. We were surrounded by all these business heads there who'd been on our flight. A hostess came up to us to ask if we were okay, and I said to her, 'You're not going to believe this. We were in a plane crash only three or four weeks ago.'

So I'm telling her the story and all the other people in the VIP lounge are listening intently.

Eventually the call came that the replacement plane had arrived and we could re-embark. As I was walking out I saw these three or four business executive dudes arguing with the hostess, and they were all wearing really stern faces. The flight took off and, when the air-hostess came around with the drinks, I asked her what the argument was about with the businessmen. She replied, 'They wouldn't get on the plane again with you lot. They say you're jinxed.'

Some time after that we were setting out for a routine band trip to the States when I found that I was personally carrying a flying jinx. As I've already mentioned, not long after I got back together with Aslan, we arranged a tour of the east coast of the States in an effort to capitalise on the following I'd built with Dignam & Goff over there. I had a permanent B2 visa, which allows you to undertake paid work in the USA. I'd been going over and back so often that they were satisfied I had no intention of staying there as an illegal immigrant.

On this trip we were going through the usual pre-immigration process at Shannon Airport, where they clear you for entry to the United States before you fly out of Ireland. I'd been through this hundreds of times before with no problem. There are four or five customs kiosks in a line to process the queues of people. As I was being checked by the fourth immigration officer in this line of kiosks, I could see along the line that the second official was looking over at me. I was passed through the inspection point, after which you walk down a long corridor into the re-boarding area at

Shannon. Myself and Joe were waiting in the re-boarding area when I saw these two guys striding in our direction. One of them was the uniformed immigration official who'd been looking at me, and the other guy was in a suit. They were still miles away, walking down a long, long corridor, but I knew straightaway they were coming for me.

The two officials brought me into an interview room and the one in the suit says, 'My colleague here saw you on a television chat show. You discussed a medical problem you had.'

'Yeah,' I said hesitantly, knowing that 'medical' meant 'drugs'. This conversation wasn't heading anywhere good.

'Did you mention your medical problem on your visa application?'

'I didn't think it was relevant. This was a problem I had years ago.'

'Did you mention it on your visa application?'

'No.'

He leafed through the documents again and said, 'Okay, go on through.'

I was very relieved, and even a bit surprised, because I knew they could be real sticklers over the tiniest detail. We arrived in the States and I was still in fear that they were going to put me on the next flight back to Ireland, but we went through with no trouble. We settled into Boston for a short stay because we had a few shows there. While we were hanging out there we went to Cape Cod for a day at the beach. It was gorgeous weather and the beach was all set up for beach volleyball, so we jumped in and played a few games. These dudes came up and offered us a game and we ended up hanging out with them for the day. That night they brought us out on the town and showed us the pubs and clubs.

A couple of days later, we were heading down to New York for our next gigs, and one of them, Brad, said he'd be in New York too. He said he knew loads of party people there and he'd love for them to look after us. So we met up with Brad and his New York mates and they brought us to all these clubs that opened until five in the morning. Some of them were real dodgy places, illegal shebeens that stay open all night fuelled on drink and coke. In the light of what happened next, we were very lucky that we never asked any of these guys if they knew where we could get a little bit of coke.

We were going into one of these clubs and I realised I'd left my bag with all my bits and pieces in Brad's car parked across the street. He gave me his keys and I pressed the fob to open the doors, and the boot opened too. I went to shut the boot and I could see a bullet-proof vest and all this cop uniform stuff. He was DEA! A Drug Enforcement Agent. They were all DEA!

And I was thinking to myself that's not a coincidence.

We'd been stopped over a drug issue at Shannon Airport a week earlier, and all the time we'd been in the States there's been drug agents with us! It was no accident that we'd run into them that day on the beach. As it happened, for the four or five days we were with Brad and his mates in New York, we'd never had even a bit of grass. Once we'd twigged the set-up, it all made sense.

I told the others about the police gear when I got into the

club, but we didn't confront Brad with it until a couple of days later. He said, sure, they were all cops, but hanging out with the band was purely an off-duty thing.

One of them gave Joe a card printed with his name and the words New York Police Department. After we got back home we rang the number on the card from the safety of Ireland. A recorded message said that the number was no longer in service.

When I got back home to my house from that trip, there was a letter waiting for me. It instructed me to bring my passport to the United States Embassy in Ballsbridge to discuss my immigration status.

I sat down with one of the embassy officials. She opened my passport at my US visa and asked straight out.

'Did you lie on your visa application?'

'No,' I said. 'All that was a long time ago. I didn't think it was relevant to now. I never had a conviction.'

'You were not asked if you had a conviction. You were asked if you have ever taken, or were ever addicted to, an illegal drug. That was the question. Did you lie when you answered that question?'

'No,' I told her. 'I did not lie. I misread or misunderstood the question.'

This to-ing and fro-ing went on for the next twenty minutes, until I said, 'Okay, maybe *technically* it's a lie ...'

And that was that.

She picked up the stamp from the desk and smacked it down on my visa: 'REVOKED'.

Anything I said after that didn't matter.

She didn't talk, she didn't listen. Good luck and goodbye.

I reapplied, and I was eventually granted a new visa, but that wasn't the end of it. Some years later Kathryn's ma was nearing the end of her life. She was in her eighties and she had a daughter in Los Angeles who she wanted to see before she died. We decided that we'd all go with her on what might be her last holiday. There was me, Kathryn, Kiera, Kiera's husband Darren and their first born, Cian. By now you could go through US immigration at Dublin Airport and not just at Shannon. So since I'd been through the process loads of times, I gathered up all the filled-in forms and handed them in to the immigration officials.

After a wait, I was called in by one of the officials.

She told me that where it asked if I'd ever been refused admission into the United States, I'd put down 'No'.

She told me that on such-and-such a date years earlier I'd had my visa revoked, which meant I'd lied on my form today.

I told her that it had happened years before, and that I'd been in and out of the States many times since.

By now, Kathryn, her ma and all the others had gone through. They were looking back at me gesturing to say, 'What's wrong?'

I waved for them to go on, that I'd sort it out and be with them in a minute.

I was wrong. Those officials are like robots. There's no reasoning with them. There's no empathy, no human engagement.

When I saw that I wasn't getting through I lost the head and went on a bit of a rant. An official asked me for an electronic fingerprint and I gave her a reply that didn't help my case.

She said, 'I know you're angry now, but you might want to travel to the United States in the future.'

I told her I never wanted to go near her kip of a country again, though I put it in stronger language than that.

I told the rest of the family to go ahead with their holiday and I'd see them when they got back. The immigration people gave me back my suitcase and I headed back to the house to fend for myself for the next two weeks. I got home and opened the suitcase and there's Kathryn's mam's knickers, corsets and the rest of her stuff. Wrong suitcase. So I was stuck at home while my good clothes, my money and my bank cards were gone west 6,000 miles.

I've never gone back to the States since.

Leaving aside my problems with the United States of America, flying anywhere long-distance has become a problem for me since I got ill. Most people will have heard of deep-vein thrombosis, which can cause dangerous clots when the body is pressurised for a long period of time. Because I have issues with my heart, I have to avoid putting it under the pressure of a long flight. The current advice from doctors is that I shouldn't risk anything longer than a four-hour flight.

And if that wasn't problematic enough, there's the additional complication of sepsis. I nearly died at the start of 2017 when my immune system collapsed, and when you're confined on a plane with hundreds of other people you're nearly guaranteed to pick up a cold or some other airborne infection. When swine flu was going around a while back I was terrified. My son-in-law Darren came over, and he had a bit of a sniffle. I told him, 'Don't come near me.' You have to watch every little thing.

40

Dicing with Death

By 2004 I was back into bad habits, only worse than ever. I kept banging up sporadically for maybe six months and then I went to a methadone clinic. I think methadone is great if it's for you, but my head wasn't in the right place at that time. I thought I needed to do something radical this time, something drastic that was going to knock me into breaking the cycle.

I told the doctor I had reservations about methadone, but I also told him that I genuinely wanted to stop. Any time I ever attempted to stop it was always a genuine attempt. I never did it to try to please anybody or to try to get back with my bird or whatever. People try for different reasons, but there is only one reason that will work for good – that you *want* to stop. So I started a methadone course, gradually reducing the dose of the heroin substitute.

I'd read everything I could on escaping addiction, because it's not a nice place. It's a horror scene. The whole lifestyle is a fucking horror scene. When you're in an addiction there's all sorts of shit happening all the time. There's all sorts of people knocking on the door at all hours, demanding money and other stuff. And by the early 2000s this was building and building and building. For me and Kathryn, our relationship was hanging by a thread. When you're strung out you're always chasing gear. Your whole life is spent out there chasing the next hit. Even when you're at home with your loved ones, you're not at home because you're hiding that other person you are, and you're hiding from those knocks on the door.

I woke up one morning in 2003 or 2004 and our two cars were smashed to bits outside. All the windows were shattered. Someone had thrown acid on the paintwork all over my car and Kathryn's car. Kathryn was freaking out. She was terrified. Little Kiera was terrified. Our family home was under attack. And me? I was looking out at the cars wrecked in the front drive and I was thinking, what's she getting so upset about? We'll get new cars. I was living in this bubble.

I went off, probably to score, and when I came back the locks were changed. Kathryn told me she'd gotten a barring order and I could fuck off. She was right. We had a young child in the house and I was bringing chaos and terror right to our front door.

I'm still trying to undo the damage that I did to Kiera throughout her life – the things I didn't do for her as a father, the times I wasn't there. You bring a child into the world and that's your responsibility. I wasn't responsible. I didn't do what I should have done. I wasn't the father I should have been. Kiera has had a lot of insecurities herself, because of me, because of the way I reared her, because of the way I treated her. I don't regret any of the things in my life really, because I don't see the point of regret – it's just a negative thing – but if I could change anything in my life it would be my relationship with Kiera. It's unforgivable, and you can't fix it, you can't undo it. You cannot un-ring that bell, and it's a burden I live with.

Today I try to have a great relationship with Kiera's kids – Cian, Ava and Jake – but there are moments when I think even that is having a detrimental effect, because sometimes I feel Kiera is looking at me saying, 'Why couldn't you have done that with me?'

Initially after I was thrown out by Kathryn, I was couch-surfing for a while. After a month or two of that I ended up in Ballymun where my sister had a flat on the sixth floor. All through that time I was still gigging with the band. When I look back now I ask myself how I was able to live through that. I remember one time leaning over the balcony of the flat in Ballymun, dropping a coin from the sixth floor and counting how long it took to hit the ground. It took one-and-a-half seconds, and I remember thinking to myself, that's all it takes. One-and-a-half seconds and you're out of here.

I look back at it now and ask myself, what the fuck was I thinking? Some of the stuff I pulled, some of the stuff I did. By now I was on crack cocaine. Unless you've experienced crack it's impossible to explain what it's like, but it boils down to this – when you're on crack, everything in your life is about the next hit. *Everything*.

When you take coke, it grips your normal state of mind and shoots it a mile high, and when you come down it brings you down a mile beneath your normal equilibrium. With crack you're increasing your pleasure a hundredfold, but the downer off it is also a hundredfold. It brings you down so far that you don't even care about getting high anymore; you just want to get back to normal. So then you take a bit of heroin to get you back to normal, because coke is speed and gear will slow you down again. I used to take the comedown gear as heroin or opioid tablets, or both. You take anything you can get because the depression is so bad. Then, as soon as you're feeling a little bit better, you want to score a bit of coke to lift the depression, and it's just a never-ending vicious cycle.

Imagine a hamster on a wheel that's flying around so fast that the hamster can't get off. That was me. As the drugs are wearing off the wheel is speeding up. Then you take the drugs and everything is in your control again, everything's cool. And while everything's cool you can do the things you have to do in your life. You can play your gigs, you can eat.

But then, gradually, as this drug is wearing off the wheel starts to go faster and faster until the ground is spinning away from under your feet again and your heart is pounding and your mind is racing and all you can think of is that you need a hit to get the wheel slowing down again.

I got to a point where I was doing so much crack that even when I was taking the drug I was getting no pleasure from it because I'm thinking, fuck, I'm going to get sick in a short while when this wears off. I need to get more drugs. The hit off heroin lasts you maybe nine hours. The high off crack lasts you thirty seconds, maybe five minutes tops. So even when you're hitting that high, you know that in five minutes you're going to be down in the pits and crowding out every other thought is that you're going to need something to get you out of that deep, sickly depression.

Incredibly, through all of this I was still turning up for gigs and somehow getting through the performances. I remember one show we played in Navan, County Meath, and by this stage I was banging gear so much that all my veins were gone, so I was skin-popping, which is where you inject it into a muscle like the doctor would do if you were getting a jab in a hospital. When you inject into your veins the heroin is straight away pushed around your body by your bloodstream, and it's cleansed as it passes through by your body's circulation system. But if you put it into a site – meaning a muscle like your arse or your thigh or your calf – any dodgy 'cut' in the heroin is going to clog at the point of injection. For instance, if the heroin is cut with cement, that cement will be trapped in the muscle at the injection point. So you end up getting abscesses.

That night in Navan I had an abscess on the outside of my thigh, and just as we were about to go on stage I pulled down my trousers in the dressing room and poked my finger at the abscess and it burst and all this pus came out in this big spurt. Tony McGuiness was getting ready next to me and he saw this and he barfed at the sight – he just threw up.

I was the walking dead, and I kept on walking. That's the absolute insanity of addiction. When you go to NA, Narcotics Anonymous, the whole thing is about the insanity of addiction, because you are, basically, *fucking insane*. When I look at my behaviour back then from where I am today, I say to myself, what was I even thinking? But nobody ever goes out and buys heroin for the first time and the next day wakes up with their body covered in abscesses. It creeps up on you.

You get your first abscess and you go, 'Holy shit! A fucking abscess! *Ugggh!*' Then you get another abscess and it's, '*Eech*, another abscess. Get on with it . . .'

And eventually they're just a minor inconvenience. I'd make regular trips to the chemist and come out with a load of pads. One time I was coming through Heathrow Airport and the security officer gave me a routine body-search. He's patting his hands down my body and he feels this bulge under my clothes, so he drags me into a room for a full search. I had to strip down for them, and when he pulled back the bandage he recoiled from what he saw – '*Awwwgggah!*' – and bundled me out of the room: 'Okay, you can go, you can go. *Go!*' Things like that happened all the time. All the time. This was now my normality.

I almost got shot in Ballymun. I was after scoring some coke to make crack. I'd got to the point where I'd buy the cocaine and I'd make the crack myself because that was cheaper. Not that it was cheap though.

I was getting lay-ons of coke from this bloke, and I owed him 800 euro. A lay-on is where someone gives you the stuff and you pay for it later. That in itself was very unusual, because when you're in that world nobody trusts anybody with credit. But this bloke trusted me, until the money I owed got to 800 quid. He was ringing and ringing and I kept telling him I've a gig on Friday and I'll pay back the lot straight after the gig. So Friday night arrived and I finished the show and saw from the missed calls that he'd been ringing me loads of times while I'd been up on stage playing with the band. I arrived back at my flat in Ballymun and the lock on the door was broken. I pushed in the door to find the bloke I owed money to waiting for me, along with another bloke who was pointing a gun at me. I handed over every penny I'd just been paid for the gig, and they left. If I'd arrived back with no money that night they would have shot me dead. That's the life I was leading day to day.

Things came to a head one day when Tony and Alan called up to collect me from the flat for a gig. Tony rang me to say they were parked outside ready to head to Drogheda. I was upstairs smoking crack with some bloke. I told Tony I'd be down in a minute. I walked down to them five minutes later with my face smashed to bits. A fight had broken out with this other crack-head in the flat over gear. He'd kicked the shit out of me.

I got into the car and Tony and Alan met me with a look of shock horror.

'What the fuck happened to you?!'

I didn't realise the state of my face. I thought I'd just got a few slaps and no one would notice. I'd gotten so used to ducking and diving from one situation to another that I thought it was just another nothing incident to get through. But my nose was splattered across my face. I was drenched in my own blood. So instead of heading to Drogheda for a gig, Tony and Alan drove me to hospital.

I'd pushed Kathryn over the brink and now I'd reached that point with the band, especially Tony. Tony told me how he would have to stand behind me on stage and look at my ribs sticking out of my back. He said, 'I can't do this anymore. This cunt's gonna drop dead any day now.'

The band always wanted the best for me outside of our life as performers. They cared for me and worried about me as a human being. So they kept giving me chances. Every time I stopped using they treated it as a line in the sand, that this would be a fresh start. There was no, 'You can't do this from now on'. They weren't watching me all the time. In retrospect some might say that maybe if they'd been stricter with me they would have made a difference, but no, they'd have made no difference. You can have all the armies of the world trying to help you, but until you want to do it yourself, none of that matters. And once you've decided that you do want it yourself, you don't really need anyone else. At the end of the day it's your battle, and yours alone.

When it comes to stopping, people expect an epiphany moment, but there's no big moment. It's a build-up of loads of little incidents like that: incidents where I got beaten up, or fell into things, or like Tony or Billy driving through town and seeing me in run-down Sean MacDermott Street in a huddle with some dodgy fuckers. Hundreds of those things.

Tony was the first to approach me about a new suggestion. He'd seen a documentary on TV about this place, the Thamkrabok Monastery in Thailand, where they treat heroin addicts. I had a vague memory that I'd seen a documentary too, maybe the same one, and there were all these kids going in, and the vibe was that if you make it through the first night then everything's gonna be cool, but the first night's going to be hard. Some of them died during their first night from withdrawal.

I went over to England and had a meeting with this charity that brought kids over to Thailand for rehab. I told them my history and they told me how the system worked between them and the monks.

I remember using heroin in the flat in Ballymun just before heading for Dublin Airport. I hooked up with the charity group in Heathrow. There were six or seven English kids going over for the same reason as me. We flew into Bangkok, by which time the gear was wearing off and I was getting withdrawal pangs. Thamkrabok Monastery Drug Treatment and Rehabilitation Centre was a couple of hours' drive north into the jungle, and by the time we reached it I was in ago-nising withdrawal – I had a fairly severe habit at the time.

One of the first things the monks did was take all our clothes off us. They gave us this uniform, a pink garment like a sarong with Thai writing on the back. They told us it said 'Patient' but I think it might have said 'Inmate'.

The vibe behind the uniform was this: because you were in this locked-down compound, if you escaped, the first village you'd come to they'd recognise you were in prison clothing. You'd get dragged straight back and your captors would probably get a little bounty prize.

I knew from day one that I was never going to try to escape. What would I do if I got out – walk all the way back to Ireland? Besides, you knew already that dressed like this you're not going to make it past the first village.

So the new intake of inmates was lined up before the abbot

and he did this blessing thing. This was followed by a little ceremony where you make commitments that you'll make an effort, and you'll try and do this and that. Then they took our passports, and they took all our money, and they gave us this Monopoly money that we could only use in the compound. The only things you could buy with it were pineapples or cigarettes or maybe some sweets.

You had to buy your food too. There was a little kitchen at the end of the big dormitory I was to stay in. I got through the first two days of withdrawal and felt slightly better to the extent that I'd try to eat something. I got an egg sandwich just to get the taste of food in my mouth, but it was covered in flies. Disgusting. All the food was disgusting, and all the food was covered with flies.

On day one I had to sign this form saying that if I died during the treatment, the monastery had no responsibility. A couple of times early on they just threw me into the dormitory and said to each other, 'This fucker's not going to make it.' They told me that near the end of my stay.

There were these two women working there. One was aged about eighty and the other was around thirty, and the pair of them used to give us Thai massages. Because heroin is a muscle relaxant, your muscles go into spasms and cramps when you're withdrawing from it. So when I was coming off the gear it was great to get a massage to ease all that muscular tension and pain. There might be ten of us waiting for a massage when the two women came around, and people would be grabbing for them, and I'd always get the eighty-year-old. Then one day I got the younger woman. When she saw the open sores all over my body she wouldn't touch me. 'No way!' Even when an abscess is gone it still takes ages for the sore to heal, and in the meantime you've another four or five coming along. The old woman was more used to this and if it wasn't for her willingness to work around the sores, I'd never have had a massage.

You don't sleep when you're going through withdrawal. I don't think I slept for most of the month I was there. For the first two weeks the withdrawals are horrendous. You don't want anyone to talk to you. You don't want anybody coming near you. You can't talk, so you couldn't even have a conversation if you wanted to. You might be able to lie down with your eyes closed, just trying to get through the next ten minutes.

If you survive the first two weeks you start to feel a little more like a human being again. You even feel well enough to take notice of the new people coming in, and you try to help them because you know what a horrible ordeal they're starting into. When I was coming towards the end of the month's stay, I started developing a bit more of a relationship with the monks, and they were telling me about the state I was in when I arrived. I had no proper memory of it because I'd been in a fever. When I first got to the monastery I was put into a dormitory and my bed had a mosquito net over it, because if I caught malaria in my condition I'd be dead. They told me that my fevered images of someone hovering over me were actually real. That was the monks leaning over me, putting a mirror up to my face to see if there was breath on the glass, to see if I was still breathing.

You always woke up coated in sweat because you were

214

in the middle of the jungle, but one time I woke up and the sweat seemed to be dribbling onto my chest. I opened my eyes and sitting on my chest was a huge praying mantis eating a cockroach. I just lay there looking at this going on, thinking I was in the horrors and this was an hallucination!

There was one dormitory for the male patients and one for the females, and the monks were very, very strict that you weren't allowed near the women. I think the reason for that is when you're strung out sex is really of no interest to you because you're in a different place. Because it's an anaesthetic drug you don't get the same feel from sex. You're kinda numb. But when you stop taking heroin your sex drive comes back with a vengeance. And the monks were well aware of this, so you weren't even allowed to walk into the women's dorm.

The patients there were mainly foreign but there were some Thais. The monks treated the locals differently to the foreigners, far more harshly. I was in one dormitory and this Thai guy was in another dorm across the way. He had a chain around his ankle attached to a lump of concrete in the shape of a bucket. He was chained into the middle of the room and we would throw cigarettes and matches to him so he could have a smoke, but when the monks returned they'd beat the shit out of him.

And I said to them, 'You're Buddhists – how can you kick the shit out of this guy?'

And they told me, 'If this guy escapes the police will just shoot him on the spot. The authorities give you one chance to redeem yourself and if you don't do it they just plug you and write down on the official report that they caught you with a gun or drugs or whatever. So their attitude was that this young fella either cleans up there in chains, or he ends up in a ditch. It's the lesser of two evils. Hardcore tough love.

During the daytime there was nothing much to do except hang around the compound. There were different things on – like drum meditations, or chant meditations – but you had a choice to take part or not. They didn't mind. The only things you *had* to do were eat and survive. I did take part in some of the stuff. One day about twenty of us were in a meditation class, and we were about halfway through it and dozing into a relaxed state, when the monks started screaming: 'Get out! Get out!' And we shot up from total meditation to total mayhem. An eight-foot-long king cobra had slithered into the room. We scattered like something out of a Vietnam War movie.

There was *one* routine that you did have to take part in. The abbot had developed this drink containing herbs and spices and the bark off trees and other stuff. It looked like black watery cowshit, and it smelled as bad.

A number of us patients would be lined up along a little gutter, each with a bucket of water and a ladle. Facing us would be an audience of local kids in their school uniforms pointing their cameras at us. Behind us there'd be monks gathered together with patients coming towards the end of their stay who didn't have to do this anymore, and they'd all be chanting loudly.

So this monk walks along the line, and he stops at each of us, fills a little cup with this black watery shit, and we have to gulp it down. So you'd try to keep that down for five minutes, ladling as much water into yourself as you could. And after five minutes of this – if you lasted five minutes – you would start projectile vomiting twenty feet into the distance. And while you're spewing out this projectile vomit, the monks behind you are chanting, '*Ya-ya, ya-ya*' while the schoolkids in front are snapping away with their cameras.

As it happened, during one of these vomit-shows there was a Channel 4 crew in the compound filming a documentary, and I'm thinking, if this ever gets shown in Ireland, I am fucked!

By the last of the four weeks I felt great though. I had a Sony Walkman, or some sort of cassette player, and there was a beat-up old guitar there, and we used to play songs. We'd play 'Yellow' by Coldplay, or Radiohead's 'Creep' – stuff like that. Just hearing music again . . . so good!

After a month was up we were released back into the outside world. I'd survived and my body was cleansed of drugs. How long before I used again? I used in Bangkok on the way home.

Myself and this young woman finished our treatment on the same day, a Wednesday. We were due to fly out of Bangkok on the Friday, so the idea was that we'd stay over in the monastery on the Thursday for safety's sake, to put temptation out of the way. But we said, 'Fuck that, we've been here for a month. Not a day longer.'

So on the Thursday the pair of us went into Bangkok and got a hotel room. There was no sexual vibe; we were just two junkies sharing. As soon as we'd dumped our stuff we got a tuk-tuk and asked the driver to take us to where we could score. The rickshaws kept bringing us to these sex clubs, and we'd pay at the door, but then we'd go through and there'd be some girl stripping and you'd tell them, 'No, not this. We don't want this. Drugs!'

We finally got to this dealer who sold us this tablet that we smoked like heroin in tinfoil. But it wasn't heroin and I got nothing off it, but that wasn't the point. It didn't matter whether it was one joint or a kilo of heroin – I'd broken the pledge I'd made on entering the monastery. When you've done that once, it's too easy to do it again and again and again …

I was out one day and already I considered the month in the monastery a failure. I flew into Dublin Airport, straight down the road to Ballymun, into a flat, and there's blokes asking 'What's it like over there?' as we're banging the gear. Straight back into it. But the monastery *had* changed me. I just couldn't enjoy it anymore. It wasn't happening for me anymore. Whatever had got into my head in Thailand stayed in my head. When I got back to Ireland I knew that something had changed, that I felt different. Before I went to Thailand I was taking gear on autopilot, but when I came back and started using again, I wasn't in that frantic, next hit mentality anymore. I'd broken that chain. I was thinking about what I was doing and I was remembering the lessons I'd learned. So something over there had entered me by osmosis, and I was never happy using again.

After a while back using in Dublin, but no longer enjoying it, I booked myself into Paddy Dunning's place, the Grouse

Lodge, in Moate, County Westmeath. It's an out-of-the-way place with apartments, a recording studio and a big old mansion house. The following year Michael Jackson and his family took the mansion for the whole summer. He must have heard I liked it. I didn't bring anything down there with me, no methadone, no anything, just cold turkey. Paddy or his wife Claire would come over every day bringing dinner for us, though for the first week I was so sick I don't think I ate anything.

I did cold turkey and, after a couple of weeks, I was okay to start up my life again. I got a little apartment in Ongar, out in the countryside on the Dublin–Meath border. I'd been there only a few weeks when Kathryn came to see me one day. Her father had passed away. I went to the funeral and after that she came up to visit me and we started talking, and we decided to give it another go.

Before that, did I think it was all over for good with Kathryn? Did I think I'd pushed her past the point where she'd never have me back?

Yes, I thought that, and at the same time I didn't know. As my habit got even worse after our break-up, there was a period when I didn't care. I put it to the back of my mind. It was always something I'd deal with later: 'As soon as I get this hit into me I'll sort that out.'

So I got clean. Kathryn took me back and we're still back. I'm still on my last chance.

Nowadays I'll open the paper and read a story about someone I would have known in Finglas who's still in that dreadful world I left behind. Some terrible incident might have happened, and Kathryn will remark that there's no way she'd be able to live like that now. Back then she was younger, and she was more in the dark about what was going on. She's now very educated about addiction. There's a support group called Nar-Anon for the spouses and families of addicts. It's about learning about addiction and fixing the damage that has been done to them throughout the addiction of their partner or parent.

Sometimes – a lot of times – when someone comes through that Nar-Anon process, they end up splitting with the addict. They think, you bastard, look what you put me through! I was your whipping boy and I never realised it until now!

Some people find that when they process all that happened, they can't find it in themselves to forgive. Fortunately for me, Kathryn had the grace to accept me back and to forgive me when she did, but she wouldn't accept it today.

41

Politics with a Small 'p'

People ask if this lyric or that lyric is political, but we've never done politics in that sense. I've tried to never demand or recommend that this is the way things should be. I've always just said how it was for me, and how I feel about it, but I've never said that anyone else should think the same way. So in that sense I don't think I've ever been a social commentator.

Take 'This Is'. 'These are the hands of a tired man'. That's about my da's hands. They were hard and calloused from work. 'This is the old man's prayer-shroud'. The shroud is the home, with all his family around him. 'These are the feet of the punished pilgrim'. These are all the pilgrims walking up Croagh Patrick, cutting their feet to shreds on the sharp rocks, and I'm thinking what a load of bollocks. God doesn't want you to do that! 'This is the face of the teenage mother'. At the time I wrote the song in the mid-'80s all the old certainties were undergoing an upheaval in Ireland. The Catholic Church was starting to loosen its grip on Irish society. Young girls were no longer shoved into laundries for being pregnant at sixteen or seventeen. You could actually have your child with you at home. All this was changing and I wanted to comment on that.

'Down On Me' from *Feel No Shame* is about sexism. I have a gay sister, Deirdre, and one day her girlfriend went into this rant at me about how I don't know what it's like to be a woman in this world. At the time I thought it was a rant, but it stuck in my mind. For the next few weeks, whenever I was in a situation, I'd ask myself if I was a woman in this situation, how would it turn out as opposed to how it did turn out today? It was a bit of an eye-opener. I came to realise that it's not the 'look at the tits on yer woman' sexism that's really dangerous. It's the insidious sexism that happens every day. It's there in little things like, 'Ma, make us a cup of tea.' You'd never say to your da, 'Da, make us a cup of tea.' So 'Down On Me' was saying, 'Don't look down on me because I'm a woman.' And by extension, it was about being Irish too, because in the 1980s the world looked down on this nation. Every English comedian still had all their 'thick Paddy' jokes. Latent racism and sexism are the same thing, and in that sense I wanted to make social commentary. But I never wanted to shove my political views down people's throats. I never said this is what we've got to do to fix it. I just painted a picture and said this is what it is. I've always admired how Bob Dylan could tear strips off the American government without ever saying the American government are a shower of bastards. He never offered solutions; he painted pictures of injustices in America. We could do with a Bob Dylan in Ireland now, because we are copying those bad American ways.

When I was a very young kid there was a fella living across the road called Dessie Querney and his ma went to

America for a holiday. Nobody in Finglas went to America for a holiday at that time. The odd person, if they were rich, got a boat to the Isle of Man for a long weekend, but nobody went to America. If you went, it was to stay. To go to America and come back was unheard of, so when she came back I remember my ma and all the oul wans on the road latching on to her for the stories. The only thing I knew about America was from *The Monkees* and *The Man from U.N.C.L.E.* and shows like that.

Mrs Querney told this story that filled us all with horror and disbelief. We couldn't grasp the concept of it. She was walking down the street in New York and there were homeless people lying in the street and she was going to give them money and the people with her said, 'Nah, walk on by, they're beggars.'

It was beyond our comprehension that anyone could just walk past a person lying on the street and treat them with such ignorance. We thought that Americans must be very hard-hearted. But here we are nearly fifty years later in Ireland and that's what we've turned into. Ireland is one of the richest countries in the world but the riches are not going where they should because Ireland is also one of the most corrupt countries in the world. There is so much to love about this country, and I was brought up to have a deep love of this land, but my loving view of Ireland was created at a time when it was a kinder place. It's that old Jesuit saying about give me the child at seven and I'll give you the man, so it's hard to change that view built in my childhood.

Sometimes, though, I have to ask myself why I love this

country so much, because I look at the resources we have, and the native intelligence we have, and the way our rugby team and our musicians and our boxers all punch so much above our weight, and then I look at the government, and the corruption in the police force, and the state of our health service and the scandalous homelessness, and it's a fucking tragedy.

You look at Ireland and you wonder why we're becoming cruel. It's because we're starting to become more educated, less ignorant and less insular than we used to be. We're seeing this dog-eat-dog, fuck everybody else mentality of the people that have a bit of power and a bit of wealth, and we're deciding that the only way to survive in this dog-eat-dog world is to copy and mimic those with power and wealth. And it doesn't have to be that way, but that's the society we're creating.

42

Marsha Hunt and Mountjoy Prison Blues

Some time after I got back from Thailand, I got a phone call out of the blue from this woman who said she was running the creative writing course at Mountjoy Prison. She told me she was bringing out a book of stories written by prisoners, and she asked if I'd like to write the foreword. I said I'd be delighted, and towards the end of the conversation I told her she had a great name – Marsha Hunt. I explained that Mick Jagger wrote 'Brown Sugar' for his girlfriend of the time, who was called Marsha Hunt.

'I am that Marsha Hunt,' she replied.

It turned out she'd been living in Ireland since the 1990s and she'd really integrated herself into the place. She contacted me in her role at Mountjoy, where she'd got ten of the prisoners to write their stories for a book. It was an esteem-building exercise for the prisoners, and it would come out in book form, so they'd have something tangible to show the world that their stories were worthwhile and as valid as anyone else's. She asked me to do the foreword because for years I'd been putting on a gig for the Mountjoy prisoners every Christmas.

Marsha mentioned that the only problem she had was with the last chapter in the book. The guy who wrote the story had since left the prison and they needed his signature on a release form before they could bring out the book. They were trying to track him down, but he was a heroin addict so he was all over the place. They could never get him at the family home.

So I got a print-out from Marsha and read it through, and I got to the last chapter. It started off along the lines of: 'I'm sitting here in the Mater Hospital handcuffed to two screws, one on either side of me, and I'm thinking that I've lost my wife and I haven't seen my daughter in so long.'

All the stories were written under pseudonyms, but I instantly knew who the writer was because I recognised the nickname he used for his little daughter. I went back to Marsha and said, 'That's Mick Penner, isn't it?'

His name was Michael Penrose. Mick was the one I'd gone to when I was trying to discover the identity of the debt collector Paschal Boland had put on my case. He was the one who told me it was Psycho. Mick has passed away now. He was a good mate of mine. The two of us used to go shoplifting together. He used to do the shoplifting and I'd drive him around the shops when I was strung out.

I knew all the places Mick might be sleeping, so I tracked him down and got him to sign the release form for the book.

He didn't last too long after he got out of jail. He tried to come off the gear but he ended up substituting it with booze and that's never a good long-term solution. He was a big Thin Lizzy fan, and he used to get a bottle of Jack Daniel's every day and just sit in his gaff drinking Jack Daniel's and listening to Thin Lizzy until eventually his liver just crashed.

Mick was a lovely bloke and a really good mate. He had a heart of gold. The reason he died so young was because he wasn't made for that world of addiction. Some people can thrive in that world, but he was too nice a person to survive there. I sang at his funeral.

I didn't stay in contact with Marsha Hunt. I still do gigs in the prison every Christmas but she hasn't been there for years. My son-in-law Darren accompanies me on guitar and we play both Mountjoy and Wheatfield Prison. I was originally asked to do it by a senior figure in the prison service, and even though I agreed straightaway, I was very apprehensive because I thought the prisoners would be real cynical and dismissive of us. The absolute opposite was the case. They're really appreciative of the fact that you've come in and you're breaking the monotony of sitting in their crappy cells all day.

The pre-gig routine for a prison is a bit different from your usual venue. You turn up, you get searched and X-rayed, they take your phones and you do the gig.

The first time I played Mountjoy was shortly after I'd split from Aslan and I was with the band I'd put together for the single 'One Man's Dream'. I was sitting on the edge of the stage talking to the audience of prisoners before the gig, and one of them asked if we could do 'Johnny B. Goode'. He was wearing prison overalls zipped up to the neck. We chatted a bit and it turned out he was in the eleventh year of a life sentence for murder. I said I didn't know all the words to the

Chuck Berry song, so I asked him if he'd like to get up and sing it with me.

We got to the end of our set, and I announced that to finish up we'd like to call up this bloke to sing 'Johnny B. Goode'. So he gets out of his seat and starts walking up to the stage and the crowd are going wild – maybe a bit more wild than you'd expect – and as he gets beside me at the mic, I notice his neck is covered in love bites. We're both standing on stage, singing into the same microphone, and he starts trying to kiss me! And the prisoners are all going mad, cheering him on! I had to get through the whole song straining my neck back. It was a gig I won't forget.

43

Triumph, Disaster, Terror, Denial, Acceptance

I've been clean of drugs for eight or ten years. I'd stopped and started over the previous thirty years, but that's when I stop-stopped. Whatever it was that eventually sank in from Thamkrabok would never allow me to use gear again. I had gained a deeper knowledge of addiction. I knew what I was doing and I knew it was a waste. Although I kept using, I wasn't getting the same out of it; it wasn't doing what it used to do, so I said to myself what's the point? That was the mental barrier overcome, but I still needed to physically get off it.

I stopped for good when a friend got me in on a methadone clinic in Blanchardstown after I'd tried everything else. The first time I tried methadone years ago I thought it wasn't the answer; that's why I went to Thamkrabok. I thought it was too cushy, but it's not cushy. You bring your tablet strength down gradually from 100 ml to 90 ml and so on over a period of time, and it's down to you what period of time that is. But the last step is the hardest, when you're going from 5 ml to nothing. You might as well be going from one thousand to nothing.

Five ml is a spoonful a day. It's nothing. But when you don't have it, it's a lot. Going onto methadone and then coming off methadone was a nightmare. But in the end that's what worked for me in Blanchardstown.

I had finally kicked the gear and I was adjusting to my new start in life when I got a bad chest infection. It went away, but then it came back and it kept coming back. From the autumn of 2011 these chest infections were persistent and my general health was really suffering. I was going over and back to the clinic at the Hermitage Centre to see consultants and they were saying you've an enlarged heart, you've pneumonia, you've this, you've that. But they weren't really getting to the core of it.

It was getting worse and worse, but it was always: 'I'll do this next gig and then I'll go back to the doctor.'

Then one day I couldn't walk up the stairs at home without having to catch my breath, wheezing. When you smoke over the years you get to the stage where you can't run around like you used to, but this wasn't like that. This wasn't gradual. This was overnight. It just hit me.

I was sitting in front of the TV and I could hardly breathe. I was gasping for breath and Kathryn said she'd had enough and she rang for an ambulance. They brought me to Blanchardstown Hospital and they put me on a heart monitor. I definitely wasn't going to make the gig booked for that weekend, and afterwards the doctor told me that if I'd tried to perform in that state I'd have dropped dead on stage. My blood pressure, my oxygen saturation levels and everything else were so low, and my heart was in such a bad way that there's no way I'd have survived. They didn't know what was wrong with me, but they knew something bad was up.

Next thing I know I'm in the intensive care cardio unit all monitored up, when I flatline. The screen above the bed is flatlining, but I'm aware of the nurses running in from the monitoring station. I'm aware there's a nurse rubbing my hand, saying, 'Christy, do you feel all right?'

I spoke to the nurse afterwards and told her that I distinctly remembered her coming in and talking to me and rubbing my hand trying to get me back. I had a PICC-line into me, a tube for getting medication and blood in and out of me. I distinctly remember them trying to get adrenaline in through that to kick-start my heart, but they couldn't because there was some blockage.

Afterwards I described all that to the nurse, and she said, 'You couldn't remember that because you weren't with us.' She told me I was clinically dead when all this was happening.

What I was seeing was like when you're a kid and you look down the silver tube of a vacuum cleaner and the light is like a kaleidoscope. There were doctors and nurses flying everywhere, ripping open syringes and boxes, and there was paper flying everywhere and it looked like confetti, and I'm lying there in the middle of this whirlwind. But I came back a little bit and I looked up at the nurse and said, 'I'm dying, amn't I?' and she just looked at me and looked away. She just rubbed my hand, and I absolutely knew.

I was filled with terror. Abject terror. I'd never known

anything like it in my life. I was just hanging on, trying to summon all my strength and make my heart pump by force of will. 'Pump ya bastard!'

They told me later that had I not lived ten minutes away from the hospital, and had my consultant not lived ten minutes away too, had all those factors not been aligned I would have died.

My consultant Doctor Galvin arrived and they moved me into another room but I was *gasp, gasp* – I couldn't get a breath into me. They were trying to get an adrenaline tube into me but they couldn't, so the next thing an anaesthetist comes in, slits my throat, and puts a defibrillator wire into my neck that kick-starts my heart. *Aaaaahhhh!* In a split second I was breathing freely again. Thanks be to Jaysus!

The next day I was taken to the Mater Hospital where they inserted a defibrillator into my chest, under the skin, which will kick in if my heart slows beyond a certain point.

Next they brought me to Beaumont Hospital for tests and biopsies to see what was going on. Doctor John Quinn examined me. He's the leading expert in Ireland on amyloidosis, which was what they suspected I had. It's a blood condition like leukaemia. The tests confirmed the amyloidosis, and at the same time I was diagnosed with multiple myeloma, which attacks the bone marrow. So they found two types of cancer in one day.

My daughter Kiera told the doctor that day that she was getting married in twelve weeks, and would I be all right for the wedding? The doctor replied, 'We don't know if he's going to make it through the next twenty-four hours. If he doesn't respond immediately to this chemotherapy, he's fucked.' He probably put it differently, but that was the message.

Even when I did make it through those twenty-four hours, I was given six months to live. A couple of years after I was diagnosed, the Sinn Féin leader Martin McGuinness died of amyloidosis. There's two versions of the disease and he had the genetic version, which in his case was specific to some related families in Donegal. They used to call it an autopsy diagnosis, because someone might die of what appears to be heart failure, and it's only when they do the autopsy that they find the root cause was amyloidosis. It's only in the last decade that medical science can diagnose it before you die and attempt to treat it.

So Doctor Quinn came to see me with the test results and says, 'Yeah, you have amyloidosis, a form of cancer.' I abused him from a height. I told him, 'You should go back to medical college and get your money back from them, man. I came in here with breathing difficulties. It's pneumonia or something. It's nothing to do with cancer.' The things I said to that man.

You go into the whole denial thing because it's so horrific. Everyone has a fear of getting cancer, but you don't ever think it'll be you. And here I was with it, and I'm going, 'Fuck! I knew, I fucking *knew* I'd get it!'

But when I was thinking all these things I was also thinking back to a year earlier when this woman rang Aslan. She told us she had an 11-year-old son in Beaumont Hospital dying of cancer. She said that he'd like to meet us, so we said we'd be delighted to say hello.

Myself and Billy got to the hospital and walked in on Steven Gerrard, who was there visiting the boy. The Liverpool captain was in Dublin doing a book promotion and he'd heard about the young fella, and he went to see him in the hospital. So when Gerrard was finished myself and Billy played a couple of songs. We went back a couple more times before he died.

So even when I was feeling really sorry for myself after getting my double cancer diagnosis, I was thinking about that 11-year-old kid. That's all he got. Eleven years. Yet there was I pitying myself after the life I've had. And that snapped me out of it. I shook myself and told myself you've done really well to get this far, considering the plane crash, the drug addictions, all these things. You're lucky to get this far.

And that's the way I started thinking. Well, Christy, you have to accept it. There's nothing you can do about it.

I spent eight months in hospital, followed by a year in a wheelchair after my discharge.

44

One Day at a Time

Everything hurts – my spleen, my kidneys, my heart, my bones. Anyone can probably see from the way I walk that I'm all out of kilter. My right hand is hanging. I can't get it to align comfortably against my side. I can't cross my legs anymore. My bones are sore. It's like having osteoporosis. My legs are sore. If I try to walk any distance they're *very* sore. Sometimes I'm in bed and I'm trying to get asleep but everything's too sore. I'd say I have the insides of a 75-year-old man, with all the wear and tear that's been done on them, and that's terrifying.

Do I ever have days when I wake up and everything is sore and I think *I can't go on*? Every day. Every day ...

Before, I never looked at life with a limit on it. Now, I start watching a TV series and I ask myself, will I make it to the end of the season? Will I be around for the finale? Dublin's footballers were playing the Quarter-Finals of the All-Ireland Championship. Is there any point in watching? Because I might not be around if they get to the Final.

That's the way it is now.

One week, two years ago, I was sailing along. It was the spring of 2017 and I played Dublin's Olympia Theatre on a

Thursday, followed by Limerick on the Saturday. Monday comes and I'm in hospital twenty-four hours from death.

It turned suddenly just like that. My body, my immune system, is so compromised and my white blood cell level is so diminished, that the least little infection can cause havoc. And that's probably what'll kill me. It probably won't be the amyloidosis or the cancer. It will most likely be an infection that does for me.

So everything I do now, if there's a big event, I try to pick the moment within that event and say to myself, 'Try to absorb this now.' Even small things like *The Late Late Show*. 'Okay, Christy, this might be the last time you're on *The Late Late Show*. Drink it all in.'

And it's horrible. I look at my grandkids and I think, will I see him making his Communion? You've never thought of those things before. You just take it for granted that you'll be there.

You'll be in bed at night . . . I was in bed the other night, couldn't sleep, and I got a pain in my heart. And I'm sitting up in bed going, 'Oh fuck. *Oooh fuck!* Here we go.'

That happens a lot. You get little tweaks and you're thinking, oh, Jaysus, is this the end now?

Or you find yourself wondering out of nowhere how the end will happen.

When I ended up in hospital after the two shows in Dublin and Limerick, I was told when I was out of danger that I'd gone into sepsis because of the infections. When I'd recovered a little, the senior nurse said that if they'd got to me twelve or twenty-four hours later I'd have gone into septic shock, and my body at that time was so weak they wouldn't have revived me.

That's how close I came that day. And if it had been left up to me I wasn't going to go in. I became incoherent sitting on the sofa, and Kathryn called an ambulance.

I've sat down a few times during my life and thought to myself that I've lived a good, full life. But I'll never forget the fear that gripped me the first time I flatlined, and the determination to hold on to life. That determination was absolute – nothing else mattered. The house didn't matter. The band didn't matter. The only thing that mattered was seeing my family again.

'I want to see my family. *Please, please, please* let me see my family again. Please don't let me die here.'

And it wasn't about dying, or going to heaven or hell or turning to nothingness. It came down to, I want to see my wife, my daughter and my grandkids just one more time.

The grandkids were up yesterday and we went out for something to eat, and the young fella, Jake, was launching himself onto my lap. He'd get off, take a run-up, and throw himself at me again. It's those moments . . . I used to let those moments pass. They were just part of life.

But they *are* life. They are the things that matter. They are the things that bring me joy, apart from being on stage. When that was happening yesterday, just playing with the kids, I was saying to myself, 'Enjoy this. Enjoy this!'

Going on stage with my weakened system there are times I just run out of energy. People ask if I can enjoy performing at all, being so run-down. But I enjoy performing now more than I ever did before, and for the same reasons that I enjoy the simple pleasures of playing with the kids. When I went through the chemo the first time, for two full years after I finished it I was still in absolute shit. What chemo does is it poisons your system. The doctors work out how much is going to kill you, and they give you a dose just below that, so they're killing everything else. Chemotherapy is very hard to explain. You feel absolutely shit – that's the only way I can explain it. I remember trying to brush my teeth and I couldn't get the rhythm. My hand was jerking all over the place. I couldn't drive. I was sitting in my car one day, stopped at traffic lights, and this car behind started beeping at me. I thought I was at home in my sitting room but I was in the car! I had to stop driving while I was undergoing chemo. So there was no joy in life. The joy was completely taken out of my life, and I was thinking, is this what I fought the cancer for, to be living like this?

For two years after the chemo, the tips of my fingers and toes were in agony, because the toxins gather at the lowest points of your body. The seizure on the Monday after the shows in the Olympia and Limerick happened because the poisons in my body reached toxic levels and it was just shutting down.

When I got ill with cancer they put me on a painkiller, oxy-codone, better known as OxyContin. It's a synthetic opiate. All these kids are getting strung out on it in America where it's known as hillbilly heroin. And they put *me* on it – can you believe it! I haven't opened the packaging. I don't take it. Then they also put me on Xanax for the anxiety. After telling me I had two forms of cancer the doctor said, 'I'm putting you on Xanax because you're losing it.'

If I went on the internet now and looked for the two prescription drugs that are causing the biggest problems for American kids at the moment, Xanax and OxyContin are the ones creating havoc. After all those years of trying to get my hands on substances like that, I'm now being given them legally, but I won't touch them. I've got prescriptions that I don't use. It's a crazy world.

45

Christy & Joe's Songs & Stories

After two years spent confined to hospital, and then a wheel-chair, I began to slowly regain my strength and some of my stamina. I still didn't have anything like the energy needed to do a full Aslan gig, but I still had bills to pay and I still wanted to sing. Myself and Joe and promoter Vinny Lawlor came up with the plan of doing an ongoing series of club gigs we call Songs & Stories. The idea was that myself and Joe would go out to local theatres with just an acoustic guitar and talk about where all these songs came from. I'd do a question and answer session, and because every audience would ask different questions, every gig would lead to different conver-sations. You'd never know what was going to happen, except that there'd always be good banter with the audience.

We're still doing the Songs & Stories shows, and they've been a huge success for us. At first it looked like it might be a disaster, though, because I wasn't sure I could get my singing back.

I was sitting at home waiting to leave for the very first Songs & Stories gig in the Draíocht Theatre in Blanchardstown, and I felt like shit warmed up. I thought of pulling out but Joe arrived and talked me into going. We were on stage that night and I was singing, but even as I was singing I was thinking I'd wasted my life. I couldn't shake these thoughts from my mind that I've spent my life as a bit-part player in something that means nothing in the bigger scheme of things – music. In my state of depression everything about me just shrank into total insignificance, and music was minuscule on the world scale of things. Everything was just diminished.

This had been my outlook for months. Music meant as much to me as table tennis. I couldn't remember that time before, when music was beautiful, when it would get the hairs on the back of my neck standing up; when I'd hear a song and say, 'Fuck, I wish I'd written that.'

But this night with Joe in the Draíocht, something happened midway through the show. I was singing, 'I have fallen down so many times . . .' and it was paint-by-numbers, no joy in it, just hitting the notes, and then, out of nowhere, the joy came back. As the gig went on I could feel my spirits rising, and I arrived home feeling really great. And that was the first time I felt well again after that two-year period of being really ill and down in myself. For the next two days I was buzzing off that gig.

Encouraged, I kept forcing myself out the door to do the shows with Joe, because even though I'd feel horrible beforehand, I felt that when I made the effort there was a great payback from it. We started putting in more gigs, just to get that buzz again. It was almost like a drug. And then it started becoming a three-day buzz, then a five-day buzz, until eventually I wasn't feeling shit anymore. It took me out of my head. I wasn't sitting there moping over how long have I left?

Before that, when I was going through that two years with the chemo in my body, I remember thinking that I'd come through addiction, I'd fought for survival and I had survived, but now my life was horrible. What's the point in it? I can't sing anymore. I'm feeling bad all the time. My memory is gone. I couldn't remember the songs.

I'd go to bed at night and the state of my mind was almost like being on acid. Chemotherapy does a lot more to you than just make you feel sick. It has a profound effect. It affects every aspect of you, like the way you think. I thought I was going mental. I couldn't speak properly. I'd go to say a word like, say, 'complicated'. I couldn't get that word out. I couldn't manage any word with more than two syllables. And I thought I was getting Alzheimer's or something like that. All these things were going through my head.

I thought I'm after going through all that to survive, but there's no quality in this. And then, when I did that first gig with Joe, a bit of quality jumped back into my life and I thought, *ooh*, that's cool!

So I built it up. Joe printed out all the lyrics and I brought along a music stand for the sheets, because when you're performing a song, if you miss out one word, while you're trying to catch up on that one word the song is passing you by and then it's gone. With the music stand I was able to reference the lyrics if I needed to. And gradually the memory came back and my voice came back.

I began to really enjoy doing the Songs & Stories gigs. It was a completely different energy. I also found a new audience. A lot of people don't come to see Aslan because they

242

have this impression – especially those from the other side of the city – that Aslan find time to do the odd song here and there between mugging old women and robbing cars. A lot of people still think Aslan are a gang of mean little thugs, and they don't come to see us because of that attitude. Throughout Aslan's career we've had to deal with that.

But from the outset we were getting a very different audience for those shows: a more varied audience. People covering a very wide age range were turning up and I really enjoyed the fact that we were reaching a new fan base. Maybe they were always there for our songs, but they never came to gigs before.

After a while, with my energy levels restored a bit, I said let's go for an Aslan gig and see what happens. We'd been missing from the gigging circuit for maybe three years and we hadn't a clue if anybody had any interest in us anymore. So we did one, and then another, and the crowds came back. I had to bring a stool on stage with me and I'd sit down a couple of times during the show. I don't run around the stage like I used to. The voice is back to the same, and the personality is back to the same, but I just wouldn't be as energetic as I used to be.

My voice has gotten deeper over the years as it has matured. It naturally gets darker as you get older, but I've never sat down and said that from now on I'm going to have to sing this way or that way. I've never had to, or tried to, modify my way of singing because of drugs or cancer or anything else. I've made no concessions. I just sing with the voice that I wake up with. I go with the changes that are naturally happening as I get older.

I think my voice now is better than it ever was simply because I'm a more experienced singer now. I've always strived to achieve excellence. I've never achieved perfection and never will achieve it, but I've always tried to achieve my very best, and I try to carry through that principle of striving every time I sing. I'm probably not hitting the highest notes I was hitting years ago with the same clarity, but by way of compensation my deeper tones are better. There's more character in them. I use what I have in me. It's a warts'n'all thing, and I've always tried to be like that.

But even with Aslan back on the road, I didn't want to stop doing Songs & Stories with Joe because I get a different payback off that. It's like having two bands, and with just me and Joe we get the chance to do a lot of more obscure material – songs we wouldn't get the chance to do with Aslan. With Aslan, people want to hear the hits and the familiar stuff. When it's just me and Joe, we can pick a lesser-known track off the second or third album. Someone recently asked for a song called 'Broken Soul'. I think it's one of the best things we've ever written, though it wouldn't be one of our best known. So when you get someone asking for that, you think, this is what I want to be doing!

46

Six Million Hits

I met Finbar Furey through the great Irish bluesman Don Baker and we just clicked. There's been two people in my life where we've just clicked straightaway, and they were the late Ronnie Drew of The Dubliners and Finbar.

With Ronnie, I mightn't see him for a year or two, but when we'd run into each other it was like we'd seen each other just yesterday. Ronnie would always have a big welcome for you. We were in RTÉ one time doing *The Late Late Show*. And myself and Ronnie were talking away in the green room. Bob Geldof was also on *The Late Late* that night. I was saying something to Ronnie and Geldof just barged straight into the conversation, cutting me off.

'How's it going, Ronnie?'

And I thought, you rude bastard!

But Ronnie just continued: 'What was that you were saying, Christy? I'll be with you in a second, Bob.'

And I thought, fair play to you, Ronnie! But that was Ronnie Drew. A true gentleman.

Finbar has a great soul. I swear to God I've never met anybody who loves music as much as him. He came up to the house when I was ill, with a banjo, and he was saying, 'Here's a song I've just written, and here's a song I have half-written.' With him it's music all the time.

I'd always wanted to do something in the traditional sense, something that was Irish. I assumed that it was never going to be commercially successful, but the intent had nothing to do with selling records, it was for me.

Doing Aslan stuff there's a pressure that goes with that. I always found it weird doing records. Your next record has to be different to your last record, but the same as your last record, because you don't want to alienate the people who bought the last one. That's a very hard line to walk. There's a lot of pressure goes with that.

But doing something traditional and Irish there were no preconditions and no expectations to meet. It just had to please me. It didn't have to be 'diddly-eye', it just had to have an Irish vein through it in some shape or form.

I played with the idea of doing something in the ancient *sean nos* style. The style I sing in, *bel canto*, is an Italian opera style that I've sort of bastardised to fit rock'n'roll. Sung in the Irish language, *sean nos* is completely different, in the way that the Irish language is completely different to English. *Sean nos* is unique in the way the singers use their runs and their trails. Everything about it is different and that intrigues me. To do justice to the *sean nos* style, you need to be seriously good.

I spoke to John Sheehan from The Dubliners about doing *sean nos* and he was full of encouragement. But I kept thinking about the singers in Mayo and Connemara, where all the good *sean nos* comes from, and these people have been learning their technique from three years of age. And here's this eejit in Dublin, who knows nothing about *sean nos* – maybe as a listener, but not as a purveyor – and I'm going to steam in and think I have a right to do a *sean nos* album. The absolute fucking cheek of you!

I've always strived for perfection in everything I've done. I've never achieved it. I never will achieve it. But I would be far from achieving it if I tried a *sean nos* album. I couldn't do it justice. It's too good, it's too profound and it's too precious to be doing a horrible bastardised version of it. So I knocked it on the head.

John Sheehan was being very supportive and he said that people would be glad that I just made the attempt, but if I can't do something really well I just don't want to do it. I still had the traditional thing in my head, though, so I mentioned this to Finbar. He told me that there's a Legend of Luke Kelly tribute concert in Vicar Street every year, and they asked me if I'd get up and do a few songs in memory of the Dubliner who died very young. So I linked up with Finbar again there, and the night was a great success.

Finbar's seventieth birthday came around in March 2017 and they asked some of his friends to join him on *The Late Late Show*. There was the then Irish football manager Martin O'Neill, the actor Patrick Bergin and me. When I arrived they suggested doing a verse of 'The Green Fields of France' with Finbar. We were doing the single verse in rehearsal and the host Ryan Tubridy told us, 'Keep going, keep going.' The floor manager was furious. He said there was only space for one verse, but Tubridy said, 'No, it's too good.' So we did a fuller version of the song live and it got a massive reaction. The last time I looked it had six million views on YouTube.

Afterwards, I said to Finbar that songs like 'The Green Fields of France' – songs with an Irish theme – were the sort of songs I'd like to do. Since then he's been writing a few songs and I've been trying to write a few songs. I want to do songs of quality.

47

Getting a Chance to Go to My Own Funeral! (Reprise)

JUNE 2013, OLYMPIA THEATRE, DUBLIN, 'A NIGHT FOR CHRISTY' FUNDRAISING CONCERT

Those covering Aslan songs, and songs associated with the band, include The Coronas' Danny O'Reilly ('Hurt Sometimes'), Horslips ('Different Man'), Mary Black and Don Mescall ('Too Late for Hallelujah'), Bressie ('Angie'), Paul Brady ('We Did'), Tom Dunne ('Rainman'), Gavin Friday ('Five Years'), Steve Wall ('Pretty Thing'), former Westlife singer Mark Feehily with the Dublin Gospel Choir ('Where's the Sun'), Jedward ('She's So Beautiful'), Damien Dempsey ('Bullets & Diamonds') and, via live-streaming from New York, U2 performing 'This Is'.

When I was very ill in hospital the first time, a friend, Deco Crawford, came up to me and said, 'What about doing a fundraiser gig? Would you have a problem with that?'

At the time I wasn't able to go out and earn, but the mortgage and bills kept coming every month. And because of the lifestyle I'd led, I didn't have a big bank account to fall back on. Kathryn had to stop working to look after me. Everything was piling up.

So I said to Deco that it would be great to get a bit of help, but I can't endorse it. I can't get involved. He was happy enough with that.

So he approached Guggi, the artist, and Guggi got in touch with the manager of Picture This, Brian Whitehead, and together they started getting together artists who were my peers. The idea was that they'd all sing Aslan songs with Aslan as the backing band.

I went along to some of the rehearsals and I really appreciated all these people giving up their spare time to turn up and rehearse. It was great fun. I was in a wheelchair. One time I tried to get up and sing something but my voice was shot from all the chemo. I couldn't hold a note. I thought my voice was gone for good, and I left that session in a terrified state.

The big night came and Brian Whitehead sent a car to pick us up. We arrived at the stage door of the Olympia and the laneway was jammed with bustling well-wishers. I'd never seen anything like it in all my years playing.

I'd always wondered what it was like to be in the audience for an Aslan gig, and now it was happening. I was sitting in one of the boxes looking down and there was a big picture of me as the backdrop – 'A Night for Christy'. I was thinking *that's* what this is . . . *this* is what they have for you when you're dead.

Nearly everybody wonders what it would be like to go to their own funeral, and to see who'd turn up and what they'd say. This was me getting the chance to go to my own funeral!

You're sitting there watching other people do your own songs. There's some songs we have that I think are really good, and there's others I wouldn't put my full weight behind now. Like, maybe we didn't really get it right there. I don't have a problem with that. You've got to try different things and that means you're going to miss the mark sometimes.

Sitting up there, hearing people taking different perspectives, I began to find different virtues in some songs that I never knew existed when I was singing them. It was a really nice feeling to hear people singing Aslan songs that I'd considered lesser songs. Paul Brady picked an obscure album track from back in the day called 'We Did', and he did a brilliant job. Mark Feehily from Westlife and the Dublin Gospel Choir did a great version of 'Where's The Sun'. There were loads of really good interpretations. And Jedward were so brilliant! Really impressive. That night changed my opinion of a lot of people.

Then, as it was coming to an end, U2 came on livestreaming from New York with a version of 'This Is'. They did a brilliant version, putting their own stamp on the song we'd written. It's not a song like 'Knockin' on Heaven's Door', that you learn in two seconds. You have to sit down and work it out, and they did. I was very impressed with that.

I kinda cried my way through that gig – it was really emotional. The crowd was looking up and clapping when there'd be little mentions and waves to me from the stage. My grandson Cian was there to take it all in. It was one of the nicest experiences I've ever had from music, after all the compromises and bullshit the business puts you through.

Even more than playing with Bowie at Slane, *this* was a golden moment.

At the end of the night I got onto the stage for the big finale. I tried to sing 'Crazy World' and it was horrendous. There's a tape of it for proof. But that didn't matter. I had my grandson Cian and my daughter Kiera on stage, and all these friends and fellow performers in the background, and it was magical, just magical.

48

Lost and Found – My Lust for Life

All the joy went out of my life for a while. After I went into hospital the first time I did eight months of chemo and they had to stop it because my body had gone toxic. It couldn't handle any more poison. I could hardly walk. I couldn't eat. But gradually it came back, that lust for life. Now I still feel like I'm eighteen in that sense.

When I was at my lowest I thought about ending it. I started to feel that I was being a burden on everybody. If I could have done it in a way that didn't bring shame on my family ... I felt that for Kathryn it was starting to drag out into a form of death by a thousand cuts. Instead of her getting one short smack of grief it was being drawn out and out, and she was on edge all the time trying to sort out every little situation. If I got a little pain in the heart she'd be on call ready to drive me to the hospital or call an ambulance. I thought her life had become one endless nightmare and I got to the point where, if I could have ended it in a subtle way that wasn't obvious, I would have done it. I just couldn't handle it anymore.

There's still the odd day when it just hits you, when feeling shite sends you into depression and the two merge into the one thing, because the minute it happens, you think it's going to be forever. You were feeling better yesterday and you might feel better tomorrow, but that doesn't matter when you feel as bad as you feel today.

When I was functioning as a drug addict, that's what would get me back to heroin. I'd feel shite and I'd go into withdrawals, and I'd tell myself I know going back to heroin now is the wrong answer to the problem, but I'll take heroin now, get myself straightened out, and then I can work out how I'm going to stop. It's easy to think that you're going to stop when you're stoned. It's the same with every addiction – drink, gambling, eating sweets. You have a feeling right now this minute and you want to change it, and you don't give a fuck, you just want to change it right now.

There were even times during my illness that I contemplated going back on the gear. I was thinking maybe if I took gear at least I'd feel better for a little while. But I kinda knew that in its essence this illness was so bad that even gear wouldn't take me out of it. Putting more toxins into my body would only make things worse.

I try now to look at everything from a glass-half-full perspective, because there's no point in looking at it in a glass-half-empty way. Taking a negative view doesn't change the thing itself. It has no benefits.

The same goes for regrets. I don't regret my life. Even the addiction. I wish that had never happened, but that's it, end of story. I don't sit and batter myself. Sometimes I do look at the years I wasted and the opportunities I wasted, and I start thinking, oh no, what a wanker. What the fuck were you thinking of? But I try to keep those moments away because there's nothing I can change about it now. All I can do is be a better person today. I've done some bad, bad shit. I haven't been the husband I could have been to Kathryn. I haven't been the best father I could have been to Kiera, and I've already explained how I feel about that. I regret that that happened with the people I love, but it happened.

That phrase 'one day at a time' gets a bad press because people associate it with giving up stuff. It's always framed to mean that something has been taken away. But one day at a time is the *only* way to live. It's about living in the moment. We can't change anything about the past and we can't really change anything about the future, because we don't know what the future will bring. It's going to be what it is. All we can do is be in the moment we're living in. If we take care of this moment, the next moment will take care of itself. Since I got sick, life has forced me to live in the present.

It's early 2019 now and David Bowie's former band played in Dublin the other night. It was a line-up of some of his greatest collaborators, including Mike Garson, Earl Slick, Carmine Rojas and Gerry Leonard. They invited me up to sing. I started into 'Five Years' and my voice wasn't there, and I told myself, 'Do this!' and I just started going for it. Because everything I do now I'm thinking this might be the last time I do it. Everything. Bowie's long-time keyboard player Mike Garson came over to me afterwards and said it was great, and we have to do it again next year, and I'm saying, 'Yeah,' but in the back of my mind I'm thinking, 'I hope I'll still be around next year, mate'.

I try to fill the time I have left with positivity and

constructive action. I'm mates with Bernard Dunne, the former world boxing champion who works with the Dublin football team as a motivation and stamina coach. Three years back Bernard got in touch and said the Dubs were doing a training camp in Maynooth and he'd like me to come and do a motivational speech for the boys.

Me, give the Dubs a motivational speech? I told him no way. I said I'd be honoured to come, but I'll just play a few songs for them.

But he insisted. He said he thought I was just the person.

So myself and Darren, my son-in-law, went to the Dubs' hotel and I gave them a bit of a talk.

It was 2016. They were on their way to beating Mayo that year after a replay to make it two All-Ireland titles in a row. They've since made it four in a row, with an eye on an unprecedented five. People are talking about them as the greatest Gaelic football team of all time. I told them they were at a point where they were winning all these trophies, and it must seem like it's going to go on forever, but it's not. 'Trust me,' I said. 'I've had moments in my life when I thought it's always going to be like this.' I told them how we toured America and I didn't take a single photograph because I'd told myself, 'Ah, sure, I'll do it on the next tour.' I told myself that this one was low key, a toe in the water. That we'd be back soon and next time we'd be dominating the place. I'd take my photographs when we were playing the stadiums. Except the next tour never happened.

So I stressed to the players that they should try to absorb the moment when they're in it. Savour it. Live in the moment.

I finished my little talk, then we played a few songs for them, and then the Dubs forward Kevin McManamon got up and played 'Crazy World' on the guitar. That was a great vibe, and we got tickets for the All-Ireland Final against Mayo. As a youngster in the 1970s I was part of Heffo's Army. We'd follow Kevin Heffernan's Dubs all over the country all through the season, to Semple Stadium in Tipperary, or Páirc Uí Chaoimh in Cork, wherever they played. Then it would come to the All-Ireland Final and during that 1970s golden era they'd usually be playing Kerry, and we could never get tickets for the biggest game of all. That completely sickened me because we were proper travelling fans. So I stopped. I never stopped being a Dublin fan but I stopped going to the games because it just wasn't fair. And, talking to people, I'm told the exact same thing is still happening today.

One of my proudest moments was when Dublin won the All-Ireland against Kerry in 2011. The Dublin players were running to Hill 16 carrying the Sam Maguire Cup, and 'Crazy World' was blasting out of the stadium's PA system, and I was sitting at home watching all this happening on TV and feeling very, very proud.

49

Three Friends Gone,
But Never Forgotten

In Aslan we've had more than our share of bad times, but the year 2017 was the worst we have ever experienced. In the space of a few months we lost Pat Fitzpatrick to cancer, and both Grace McDermott and Svenn Braamark in tragic fires. They were three very special individuals and not a day goes by that we don't feel their loss.

Svenn turned everything around for us. He transformed our whole way of thinking about ourselves. Before Svenn arrived on the scene, we had gotten ourselves into an unhealthy rut, playing the pub circuit we thought we'd long left behind us. It was earning us a living, but we were travelling in ever-decreasing circles.

Over time we got to a stage where people were saying, 'Ah, we won't go see Aslan tonight because they'll be playing somewhere nearby next week and we can go and see them then.' Familiarity bred contempt, and we arrived at a situation where they weren't coming to see us any week because we were so available.

Then along came Svenn and he changed everything.

Svenn came to Ireland to open a head office here for the charity Cradle, which he had founded. Before arriving in Ireland he'd been an aid worker in a number of war zones. During the Bosnian War of the early 1990s, Svenn would get a truck, and he'd fill it full of food and medicines and drive into Bosnia's war zones. His focus was to bring food and medication to kids caught up in the fighting. It was only after he passed away that I realised the extent to which he was involved in this emergency work. I knew he ran the charity, but I'd assumed he ran it from behind a desk. Not so. He was totally hands-on. There's one video I've seen where Svenn drives up to a checkpoint, and one of the warlords demands to know who the supplies are for: Muslims or Christians?

Svenn says, 'It's for children.'

This warlord was threatening to blow his head off, but Svenn faced him down. He was an incredibly brave man.

When the war ended in Bosnia, Svenn came to Ireland and based the headquarters of his Cradle charity in Dublin. He continued to generate funds to send over to Bosnia to rehabilitate the children as the country rebuilt itself.

In July 2011 Anders Behring Breivik slaughtered seventy-seven people in Norway, most of them kids at a summer youth camp. Svenn came to us in the wake of the massacre and asked us if we'd give him the use of 'Crazy World' to help raise funds for the survivors. After that he just started hanging around and turning up at gigs. At first, he seemed to be at every gig we played, then he started getting involved, helping us out on a casual basis. When we'd arrive for a gig he'd have our hotels sorted for us. He was like a tour manager.

After years of bad management, followed by more years of managing ourselves, finally this bloke had come along who was willing to take charge and who had our interests wholly at heart. On a personal note, he also started building up my confidence by the simple measure of treating me with respect. He gave us a value of ourselves, as a band and as individuals. He thought we were the best band in the world that hadn't been discovered. He had that attitude towards us and he instilled that attitude back into us. That level of self-belief had been beaten out of us over the years, to the point we had almost become a pub-rock band. We *had* become a pub-rock band. Svenn lifted us out of that. He made us believe again that we are better than this!

Svenn then started looking at the sort of gigs we were playing. He told us we were diluting ourselves by playing every toilet in the country. Svenn would ring our agent and query the fee we were getting, and if he didn't think it reflected our worth he'd tell them to come up with a better fee or cancel the gig. And if he was told there was no moving on the money, he'd say fuck them. So he cut out all these pub gigs. We weren't gigging as much, but we were getting paid much better for the ones we did play. He got all our finances together.

Svenn was an accountant by trade, and he started examining our contracts. He found clauses in them that we didn't know were there, and he'd go to the record labels and publishing companies and point out that if they hadn't taken up this option or that option within a certain time, the rights reverted back to the band. In that way he started getting our music back into our ownership. In situations where we were getting 10 per cent of our royalties and the record company was keeping the other 90 per cent, we were now getting 100 per cent of what was due to us. Until Svenn arrived we had no idea what we were earning. Most of it was going to other people. Svenn was doing all this for us but he'd never let us pay him. We wanted to give him a wage but he wouldn't take a penny. It was a labour of love for him.

Svenn didn't need our money. He had a huge forest farm in Sweden from which he financed his lifestyle and his activities. He'd go over to his farm for a couple of months every summer and chop down a load of trees and sell the timber.

In May of 2017 we played the Opera House in Cork, and we were booked to play a private party in Waterford a couple of days later for a Canadian millionaire. The party host had rented out an entire hotel on an island, and all the guests flew in from Canada to Dublin and then had a helicopter race to Waterford. The bash was for the millionaire's wife. She'd seen us on *The Late Late Show* and loved us, so we got the invitation to play at her birthday party. Svenn said that he didn't need to be there for a private gig, so he was going to head over to his farm in Sweden, tidy up some business there, and he'd see us the following week.

So that was it. 'See you next week, Svenn.' And we never saw him again.

Svenn went back to his farm. His neighbours were scorching the earth, where you burn back the foliage so you get better growth for the new shoots. The winds turned unexpectedly and the flames started blowing towards Svenn's farm. He was running in and out, throwing buckets of water, trying to get a firebreak between the fire and his trees. The exertion got to him and he had a heart attack. The heart attack didn't kill him, but he had to sit down. It took the others half an hour to find him, and all this time he'd been collapsed there breathing in thick smoke. They rushed him to hospital and induced a coma because of all the damage the smoke had done to his lungs and his brain. They kept him in a coma for two weeks, and we all assumed that he'd be grand. We thought it might take some time, but he'd recover. We never thought for a second that that was it. They took him out of the coma and he was brain dead.

I was devastated. To this day I'm devastated. As I've said, Svenn was one of three great people we lost in a horrendous 2017, who all died long before their time. Shortly before Svenn we lost Pat Fitzpatrick, 'Fitzy', to cancer. He'd made himself indispensable to the band. Back in 1999 we decided to get in a string section for the recording of our live album, *Made in Dublin*, at Vicar Street. Fitzy was able to score the string arrangements onto sheet music for the orchestral players. That was the first time we'd used him, and for a while we'd just get him in for special occasions. Like, if you were going to do a TV performance and you wanted to do something classy, you'd get Fitzy in to play the piano. But then, when we took him out of the Aslan line-up, I felt we lacked something, because he was such a brilliant musician and a lovely, lovely person to have around. The gigs were just not as good without him. To me it has always been about trying to make the best of what we have, and with Fitzy on board, Aslan were better. So he became a full-time member of the band for over ten years. He was diagnosed with cancer around the same time I was, and I had no doubt that I was going to be the first to go. It didn't work out that way. He's sadly missed.

Then, at almost the same time, we lost Grace McDermott, who did our social media. Grace was only twenty-six when she died tragically. She went down to Limerick to take part in the Great Limerick Run. She bumped into this mate of hers down there and decided to stay overnight on his couch. He told her she could have his bed and he'd sleep on the couch. A fire started in the middle of the night. The inquest couldn't find for definite what started it, but the house was filled with carbon monoxide. The fire brigade arrived and dragged them all out, but Grace's friend, who'd swapped his bed for the couch, was unconscious with the fumes, and he was the only one that knew Grace was in the house. The fire brigade thought they'd pulled everyone out, but Grace died in the blaze.

I didn't know Grace very well, but for her to be taken away so suddenly, so young and so full of life, was heartbreaking for us all. With Fitzy, he'd been ill for two years after his diagnosis, so he had time to prepare himself. Not that that made it any easier for him, but having that time to say your goodbyes is something worth having. With Svenn it was 'see ya next week' and then never seeing him again.

A year after Svenn's death we were playing Cork Opera House again, which is where we'd said our last goodbye to him. We did Pink Floyd's 'Wish You Were Here' in his memory, and I told the audience what had happened. I've only ever lost it on stage twice. The first time was when I broke down singing 'Crazy World' looking at Kathryn from the stage, and this was the second. I was just hit with this devastating sense of loss and I had to stop singing.

In a career as long as ours, you meet thousands of music biz promoters, journalists, disc jockeys, managers, agents and hangers-on. Every one of them has an agenda. Every one of them is looking for something. Svenn was the exception. He had no agenda, no ulterior motives. What he did he did out of the goodness of his heart. He did so much for us and he wanted nothing in return. He didn't even want the kudos. He didn't put himself out there as the man who'd done all these things for Aslan. Every one of us in the band is still devastated. All death is final, but with Svenn it was *bang*, he's gone. We never got a chance to say goodbye, but what's worse is that we never got to sit down and tell him how deeply we appreciated what he'd done for us.

Svenn's legacy to us is that he reinvented Aslan. When he came to us first, we were going nowhere on the poky pub circuit. Thanks to him we're back on top. For instance, for the past few years a fixture of our summer has been selling out the Iveagh Gardens festival venue in the centre of Dublin. I don't remember any time when the Aslan brand was bigger than it is now.

I think that when people looked at us again they saw quality and commitment and perseverance and character, and I think people appreciate that. We have written and recorded two classic Irish songs in 'This Is' and 'Crazy World', and they will still be played and sung for many years to come.

'Crazy World' has been all over the TV and radio for years now as the theme song for an insurance company advert. I can't explain what it does for me hearing it as part of the soundtrack of life in Ireland, but it's a nice vibe. Fame for me is a real strange animal, because you're only famous in patches. You release a record and you're on TV and the record is being played on the radio and you're famous for that moment. But as the airplay of the record diminishes, so your fame diminishes – not in your head, but in reality. You're invited to fewer launches. Fewer people want your autograph or your photograph. Then you have another hit and you're famous again until it fades again. You're up and down, in and out, famous and not famous. But with something like the advert, that's where you're right into the Irish consciousness.

I did the comedian Tommy Tiernan's show and he said, 'Do you realise that two songs you've written have become part of the Irish DNA?' He meant 'This Is' and 'Crazy World'. I'd never thought of it that way. But once he said it I realised that I'd had that same feeling whenever that ad came on, though I couldn't articulate it. But that's what it is. Aslan have buried themselves into the psyche of the Irish people. That's what I think when I watch that ad now. And I obviously think of the money ...

'Crazy World' was not written for Kathryn or for Kiera. It's just a response to the madness and uncertainty that we all have to face in our day-to-day living.

When I look at my grandkids, Cian, Ava and Jake, I'm afraid for them in the world they're going into. People call it progress, but I don't see any redeeming features in it. To me, everything is getting worse. Everything is getting harder.

I was educated in Patrician Brothers, which was the most academic school in Finglas, and we were trained to understand that if we did a really good Leaving Certificate we would be able to get a solid civil service job for life. As the epitome of our aspirations it was a very modest one, but at least it offered a decent future. In my case, I wasn't interested in that because I was set on music. Nowadays there isn't even a guarantee anymore that if you work really hard at school you can have a steady boring job. And as for trying to make a living from music – that's got even harder.

What Bob Dylan said about the music biz a long time ago now seems to apply to everything. He said that the music business is like a joint of meat, and everybody takes their slice before you get to the essence of the thing, which is the music and the music maker. Nowadays, no matter what your enterprise, there's more people taking their slice, there's more obstacles. Life really has got harder.

I consider myself lucky that I was born into a beautiful Ireland and into a beautiful world, but I've lived to see the demise of that beautiful world. I don't know if my parents came, or if every generation comes, to feel the way that I feel today, but I don't think so. I think it's gone bad. I'm not a religious person, but there is a certain spirituality, a certain decency, a certain integrity that we had as a nation that is being eroded. Every day I see less and less and less of it. It's nothing to do with foreign people coming in or anything like that. We're doing it to ourselves and it's heartbreaking to see.

When I go away for any period of time I'm dying to come home. I love arriving into Dublin Airport, or even just driving up the Naas Road coming home from a country gig, and seeing certain sights that let you know you're back in Dublin. There used to be a natural elation about coming home, but increasingly I have to remind myself what it is I like about coming home, and basically it's family. That's all that's left now. There's very little societal-wise, and that's heartbreaking because we're so much more than that as a nation.

What's most terrifying about the way we're changing for the worse is how fast it's happening. The computer has had the same effect on society as the arrival of the railways almost 200 years ago. Before the train, most people who lived inland from the coast never tasted cod or mackerel. With the coming of the railways, you could transport all sorts of fresh food deep into the country for the first time in history. But with the train came train timetables, and with train timetables you got clocks everywhere all set to the same time. Before the trains, every town and village ran to its own time set to the midday sun. Every community lived at its own pace. So you can compare the computer to the railways, but multiplied 100 times. Life has changed more in the last fifty years than in the previous 500, and it's still changing so fast it's hard for people to keep pace. People are trying so desperately to hang on to what they have that they don't give a fuck who they hurt in order to hang on to it. I see the rise of populism and right-wing politics as a repeat of what happened leading up to the Second World War. You think of Hitler saying, 'Make Germany great again', and it's exactly what Trump is saying about America. The mentality is the same. Eighty years apart but the same, as if no lessons have been learned.

We need a revolution, like the French Revolution. The French have a great attitude. They don't take no shit from their politicians. Go outside their cities and they have a great way of life. They've held on to their culture, which has a lot to do with holding on to their language, and it's a great culture. The French are holding out against becoming Americanised. Ireland *is* Americanised.

50

If I've Left Out Certain Things . . .

All of us are an accumulation of our experiences during our lifetimes. I've told my story here – it doesn't come with a moral to it. I don't know if there should be a moral to it. It's just the story of my life.

If I wanted to achieve anything it has been to show that good stuff does come from working-class parts of Ireland, of Dublin, and from Finglas in particular.

I've tried to be totally honest throughout my life and it's gotten me into trouble over the years. I've been recklessly honest. I've said a lot of things I shouldn't have said.

Some people think I'm in the business of creating my own myth, but that's not true. To set up your own narrative you'd have to polish things up and I've never done that. In fact, if anything, I've toned things down. The only way I've made up my own narrative is in the sense that I haven't included all the things I've done. But if I've left out certain things it's not to show myself in a shining light – it's to avoid causing hurt to certain people and, in a couple of cases, to save myself from going to prison.

Writing this in the spring of 2019 I'm in a good place, given all the circumstances. Musically I've reached a plateau where

I can pick and choose the gigs I want to do. I love Aslan. The rock'n'roll thing still works for me. But when it's just me and Joe on the stage there's a totally different energy. As a singer that pairing works great, because I can properly sing. When we play in a theatre, you can hear a pin drop. You're not competing with drums or guitars or keyboards. So I love being able to actually sing, and we can still go out with Aslan and do the rock'n'roll stuff. So it's like being in two bands: the best of both musical worlds.

There's never been a master plan, no long-term plan, just put one foot in front of the other, get to tomorrow and see what happens. The story of my life, and of everyone's life, I'm sure, is that you make insignificant little decisions that have all sorts of unintended consequences. Anyone who claims they've followed a master plan through life is lying. People fill in the master plan with the benefit of hindsight, after the random events have played out. There are people who are, say, doctors now and they'll tell you, 'I went to college and studied hard and became a doctor. You didn't become a doctor because you were out partying all the time.' If they were honest they'd have to admit that they were born into a family who could afford to send them to a great school and then to a great college, and who could count on giving their offspring great social contacts and job opportunities. I often wonder how many champion showjumpers, how many world-class golfers and how many top tennis players were born in Finglas that were never discovered because they weren't exposed to showjumping or golf or never saw the inside of a tennis court.

If I have had one goal it was, and is, to leave things better than I found them, and to give something more to Kiera and her kids than I had; to give them a better start than I had.

I cradled Kiera on the cover of *Feel No Shame* when she was eighteen months of age. I held her in my arms again to wave to the crowd at our reunion gig in 1993, but I never encouraged her to go on the stage as a performer. I didn't hear her singing until she was fourteen. Kathryn used to say to me that Kiera had a lovely voice, and I'd say to Kiera, 'Sing us a song,' but she wouldn't sing – that's how kids are. Then, when she was fourteen, we were in Portugal and we went to this bar with a karaoke machine and she got up and sang. That was the first time I ever heard her sing. I offered to give her singing lessons but she had no interest – it wasn't that she had no interest in singing, but she just wouldn't do it with me. She has a band together now but she doesn't want to be getting gigs and TV slots off my back. She's her own woman.

Kiera is a great young one and she's a great mother to Cian, who's now fifteen, Ava who's eleven and Jake who's five. I spend as much time with them as I can. I wanted a big family. I was one of eight kids and Kathryn was one of ten, so we both came from big families and we both wanted loads of kids but it just didn't work out that way. Kathryn had three miscarriages and then got cervical cancer shortly after Kiera was born, so it just happened that way. Now, with Kiera's kids, as any grandparent will tell you, it's a second chance for us. With your own kids you have to temper how you treat them with your wisdom of the world, and with discipline and all those things. With your grandkids, all that goes out the window: 'You want sweets? Have some sweets!' They're great. I love them. We babysit them most weekends when Kiera's gigging and I'm not gigging. Even if I'm gigging I'll come back late and they'll be staying overnight so I'll see them for breakfast. I bring Ava horse-riding every Sunday because she's mad into that. Cian is a Dublin boxing champion and Jake is still a lovely little kid.

Kiera's husband Darren is my sometime musical partner. Kiera met him when he was the guitarist in a band called No Angels. I was helping them out and Kiera started doing backing vocals. Shit happened and she got pregnant, and I thought, the bastard!, but he's turned out to be a great guy. Darren's a real hard worker. By day he's a bus driver, and by night he runs the band for Kiera. He's just a great husband and father – a really, really good guy. One of your biggest wishes on earth is that your child marries someone decent, and I've been very lucky in that sense.

Everyone sets out to live a life. For me, it seems I had to live an autobiography. I'd never recommend doing what I've done. Some of it was horrific. *Horrific*. But it was a wild education. I've seen some things and I've done some things. I've seen some lifestyles and I've led some lifestyles, and I've met some people that I'd never have been exposed to if I'd kept to the straight and narrow. That's been a great education in life, but not the sort of education I'd recommend to anyone. I would not say to anybody, 'Go ahead with that life and you'll arrive happily where I'm at today.' Because 99 per cent of people who've lived my kind of life are either dead or in jail by now.

I worked in the phone company, Telecom Eireann, and

there's people I worked with there who retired early and are now enjoying life on their gold-plated state pensions. I was talking to one of them recently and I said, 'There you are, you jammy bastard. I'm the one who walked away from that job to be a rock star, and there you are now living a life of the idle rich while I'm still out there slogging away doing gigs to make a living.'

And he said to me, 'Yeah, but look at the life you've had. I've had to get up at seven o'clock every morning for forty years to go to work at something I don't particularly like.'

And I could never have done that. I was never made to do forty years in a nine-to-five. Tell me to do something, or ask me the wrong way, and I react. Maybe it's my self-esteem issues, but taking orders always grated with me. I already felt less-than, so when bosses would treat me in a subservient manner, it would just grind on me.

The person in my life who has always made me feel more-than is Kathryn. Kathryn is an amazing person. She has this great inner strength. Her parents were brilliant parents, and she's a testament to how good they were. Of all the things I've fucked up in my life, I've made one good decision, and that was Kathryn. The gods were smiling down on me the day I found her. I could not have survived as a person without her. When I got ill she was back in there again, taking care of me, taking care of everything.

I don't know how she does it. I've said before that if the roles had been reversed, I don't know if I would have had the strength of character to put up with what she put up with. She has told me that, with every crisis I've gone through in my life, she always had faith that I would come back to being the person she fell in love with. No matter how bad things got, Kathryn always believed that that person would come back to her. She feels now, after all these years, that that has happened, that I've come back.

We're in a great place now but, Jaysus Christ, we've gone through a lot to get here. As a journey, I wouldn't recommend it.

I don't know anybody else who's gone through what I've gone through and has survived to come out the other end with any worth in their life. I've been a jammy bastard throughout my life and it has nothing to do with strength of character. It's to do with the fact that Kathryn has always been there for me. She has been my backbone and my luck.

Sometimes I sit back and look at the achievements of Aslan, and of me as a singer, and I ask myself should I be happy with the level of success I've had, or should I feel hard done by, or should I feel that I've failed? I always come around to the same answer. From the age of fifteen I had these ideals and dreams and visions of what I wanted to be as a singer. As I was progressing through the music industry I found that there are certain compromises that you have to make to get to the next level. There were many compromises I was not willing to make, and which to this day I am not willing to make. I've arrived at a place where I'm doing something that I love doing, and I feel that I'm doing it at a credible level. I have my singing, my home and my family, and that for me is the perfect balance.

And I never sold my soul.

ACKNOWLEDGEMENTS

For the lads from Aslan: Joe Jewell, Billy McGuinness, Alan Downey, Rod O'Brien and Mark Redmond. Special thanks to Eugene Connolly, Denise McCormack, Smokey, Archie, Mark Downey and Mairin at *Hot Press*. With deep gratitude to the public who have stuck with me through thick and thin. My love goes to my family: Kathryn, Kiera, Darren, Cian, Ava and Jake.

INDEX